A Special Education

A SPECIAL EDUCATION

One Family's Journey through the Maze of Learning Disabilities

DANA BUCHMAN

with Charlotte Farber

Da Capo

LIFE
LONG

A Member of the Perseus Books Group

Text designed by Jeff Williams
Set in 11.5-point Electra by the Perseus Books Group

Library of Congress Cataloging-in-Publication data
Buchman, Dana.
    A special education : one family's journey through the maze of learning disabilities / Dana Buchman with Charlotte Farber.—1st Da Capo Press ed.
        p. cm.
    ISBN-13: 978-0-7382-1033-9 (hardcover : alk. paper)
    ISBN-10: 0-7382-1033-1 (hardcover : alk. paper) 1. Buchman, Dana. 2. Farber, Charlotte. 3. Parents of children with disabilities—United States—Biography. 4. Learning disabled children—United States—Biography. 5. Mothers and daughters—United States—Case studies. 6. Learning disabilities. I. Farber, Charlotte. II. Title.
    HQ759.913.B82 2006
    306.874'3087—dc22
                                                                                        2005035779
First Da Capo Press edition 2006

Published by Da Capo Press
A member of the Perseus Books Group
http://www.dacapopress.com

Da Capo Press books are available at special discounts for bulk purchases in the U.S. by corporations, institutions, and other organizations. For more information, please contact the Special Markets Department at the Perseus Books Group, 11 Cambridge Center, Cambridge, MA 02142, or call (800) 255-1514 or (617) 252-5298, or e-mail special.markets@perseusbooks.com.

3 4 5 6 7 8 9—09 08 07 06

INTR✳DUCTION

ONCE UPON A TIME, I WAS PERFECTLY BEHAVED. I juggled marriage, a fast-paced career as an emerging fashion designer, and motherhood, all with a perpetual smile on my face and nary a complaint. I lived in a constant state of emergency, barely sleeping at night. I exhibited emotional needs rarely (and grudgingly). I kept my fears and doubts politely to myself. And I never, *ever* displayed a trace of anger.

I was, in a word, a time bomb.

Then, as if everything I was balancing in mid-air weren't enough, I found out that our eldest daughter, Charlotte, had severe "learning disabilities" that might affect not only her schoolwork but her ability to function in the real world as well. She turned out to be dyslexic, had trouble counting, couldn't tell a story, moved awkwardly, lacked fine motor skills, and had absolutely no sense of direction.

This is when I started to lose it.

Unless you also have a child with what we've since learned to call *learning differences* (LD) or other major differences, you can't imagine the impact these issues have not just on your child but on you and the rest of your family. This is what it's like:

It begins with noticing that your little bundle of joy isn't doing everything he or she is supposed to do on schedule according to the baby manual—cause for a first-time parent's total freak-out. You seek out the help of doctors and other professionals, get a diagnosis—and things just get more confusing. You don't know what on earth it all means, whether it reflects on you as a parent, or how to help your child because there is so much vague and conflicting information out there. You continue seeking the help of professionals, spending hours and perhaps lots of money each week at tutors and specialized therapists. In the course of it all, you get stuck in the mind-set of "fixing" your child.

You also endure the heartache of watching your child struggle in ways other children—including *your* other children—don't, and often publicly. You see your other children grapple with complicated emotions, and you struggle to distribute your attention fairly. You make a lot of mistakes—you have your own learning difference when it comes to understanding LD and knowing how to help your child. And you're constantly flooded with feelings of disappointment, guilt, embarrassment for your child, shame, fear for the future. It's a lot to deal with.

For me, it ultimately had the effect of upsetting my perfectly arranged little applecart. What astounds me now is that this extremely painful and difficult upset turned out to have been a very good thing. It led me to a less "perfect" and more authentic version of myself. I've realized that Charlotte and her LD have been catalysts for my personal growth and my more holistic, positive approach toward life.

If it weren't for Charlotte and the hurdles posed by her LD, I would not have been pushed to the point that I had no choice

C✸NTENTS

ACKN✺WLEDGMENTS

I WOULD LIKE TO THANK SARI BOTTON FOR GIVING order to my thoughts and giving voice to my feelings.

Also to my agent, Faye Bender, for believing in the project.

And to my wonderful editor at Da Capo Press, Marnie Cochran.

To all my colleagues and dear friends at Dana Buchman, especially Shaun Glazier, for pushing me to go forward.

Thanks to Charlotte's three fabulous schools—The Gateway School, Stephen Gaynor School, and The Churchill School and Center—and especially to the wonderful educators who have taught Charlotte and me so much.

My deep gratitude goes to the tremendous professionals who have helped us all along the way: Leda Molly, a brilliant speech therapist and our family LD coach; Monica Lowe, the fifth member of our family; Dr. Michele Shackelford, for early intervention; Dr. Richard Fischer; Chris Legrand; Toby Pulanco; Dr. Carole Grand; Loren Stell; Claudia Becker; Glenn Corwin; Sridhar Nagubandi; Dr. Anita Dick; Miki

Huber; Scott Gaynor; Yvette Siegel; Dr. Joyce Pickering; Amy Rosenthal and Jan Benson.

Also, to my brother Jim Buchman, sister Leslie Richardson, and loving in-laws.

Thanks to my sweet family, my darling hot stuff daughter Annie Rose, and the dream of my life, my husband, Tom Farber.

And, finally, to Charlotte, for her hard work, inspiration, contribution to the book . . . and to my life.

but to face my tightly contained emotions. It was only through managing Charlotte's LD that I would realize how much help I personally needed, not only with taking care of Charlotte but with things that had nothing to do with Charlotte and her LD, things her LD helped me to discover within myself. I needed to uncover and examine those parts of me that were prejudiced, bottled up, and perpetually anxious.

If it weren't for Charlotte, who wears her emotions and her vulnerability on the outside, unedited, for all the world to see, I might never have learned to express my own feelings. Also, if it weren't for Charlotte, the whole family—my husband, Tom, my younger daughter, Annie, and I—would have maintained very narrow views of intelligence and success. We wouldn't have been inspired by Charlotte's incredible perseverance when the odds were against her or her boundless compassion for others who struggle in life. Nor would we—three Type A go-getters—have learned to slow down and tune in to ourselves and the people close to us through Charlotte's example. What's more, we would have missed out on the closeness we have all gained from going through this eye-opening experience together.

That said, I would be lying if I claimed it was easy. It hasn't been, for any of us. Having LD, having a child with LD, or having a sibling with LD is extremely challenging on many levels and, at times, very painful. But the Buddhists say that pain is your teacher, your friend. It's what brings you to greater awareness in life and, ultimately, to greater happiness, if you're willing to learn from it. And I've been learning that that's true.

For all that Charlotte and I have been through, I now feel more awake and aware than ever before. I am optimistic about Charlotte and her future. She is too. And watching Charlotte has inspired me to appreciate better every aspect of my life—my family, my marriage, my health, and my career success.

I'm still pretty well behaved, but I live less rigidly, and more and more often, I speak up and tell people when I'm angry. Life is a little less controlled, a bit messier—and that's a good thing. It's been a long, bumpy road to where I am now, but I wouldn't trade this experience for anything, and, I think, neither would Charlotte.

Chapter 1

THE WONDER YEAR

SOME PEOPLE, WHEN FACED WITH A MAJOR LIFE change, make a conscious effort to slow everything else down. A woman who's having a child for the first time might decide to lighten her load at work. Someone who is taking on new responsibilities in her job might hold off on starting a family that year.

I have never been one of those people.

For most of my life, I have been a serious doer, undaunted by the notion of having too much on my plate. If anything, I would jump at the chance to juggle more for all the world to see. I had been encouraged early on by my mother and my grandmother to be a high achiever, and I got hooked on the accolades they showered on me. I wanted to be a superwoman, the embodiment of the "having-it-all" feminist ideal that became so popular when I was in college in the 1970s.

If there was ever a year when I got to shine, it was 1986, probably the most action-packed and thrilling year of my life. I did it all then: I was newly married to my husband, Tom; we had our first daughter, Charlotte; and the Dana Buchman designer label was born. I had everything I had ever wanted. It was a series of dreams come true. I had this amazing husband—not only handsome but brilliant, loving, and supportive of my career! Then, I received the offer of a lifetime for a young designer, the chance to have my own label. It was practically handed to me on a silver platter by my mentor and boss, Liz Claiborne. (The Dana Buchman label is owned by Liz Claiborne, Inc.) To top it all off, I gave birth to this perfect, beautiful little creature whom I just loved instantly.

Could it get any better? My life was picture-perfect—on the outside, at least. People thought, *Look at her, keeping it all together, doing everything at once with so much grace and style.*

On the inside, though, I was a bit of a mess, and I didn't even know it. I was so out of touch with my emotions, so into living the dream and seeming "perfect," that I don't think I even knew how overwhelming it all was. Here I was, under tremendous pressure to prove myself in designing my first collection, and at the same time, I was just learning how to care for a baby. These were two insanely demanding endeavors unto themselves, let alone in combination.

It was in the next year, when Tom and I started to notice that there was something amiss with Charlotte and her development, that it started becoming harder for me to hold it all together. The idyllic picture of my "perfect" life began to pixelate like a frozen image when the DVD player gets stuck. In the years that followed, that picture would take on a different hue, colored by the experience of having a child with serious learning differences (LD) and motor deficiencies.

THAT GIRL FROM MEMPHIS

My adult life has been shaped by many things. Being the mother of a child with LD has turned out to be one of the major, defining details. It's been a rigorous education—nineteen years and counting. And now it's hard to recall a time when LD-speak wasn't a part of my vocabulary.

Growing up in Memphis, Tennessee, in the 1950s and 1960s, I can assure you I never heard the term *learning difference*, or even the less politically correct *learning disability*. Back then, unfortunately, the kids who had difficulty reading and spelling and doing math were labeled "the dumb kids." Knowing what I do now about LD—how it is the result of different brain wiring rather than a lack of intelligence—I tend to think many of those kids were probably pretty bright, and it breaks my heart to think of the kids I and others judged unfairly.

Me, I was always near the top of the class, an A student who loved sitting at the front of the classroom, raising my hand for the teacher to call on me. I was the youngest of three kids in a family that placed a high value on academic achievement.

My mother never worked but was an avid reader. I remember her reading Plato when I was quite young, telling us to be quiet because it was very difficult. At one point, she offered to pay me $50 if I'd read Shelby Foote's *The Civil War* (I did!), but bribing me was rare; mainly she just inspired me to read by her example. At sixty, she enrolled in Memphis State University to get her master's degree in English. I was an undergraduate English major at Brown University at the time and had just learned to write papers. Ironically, my mother would send hers to me for guidance and correction. From my father, I got a strong—almost fierce—work ethic. A child of the Great Depression, "Whirly," as I called him once I got too old for "Daddy," worked very hard. He was a co-owner of a steel-fabricating plant. The plant opened at 7 a.m., and my dad was there, right on time, every morning. My parents awoke at 5:30 a.m., and at 6 a.m., my mother brought breakfast upstairs on a tray. We kids were always welcome to join them for breakfast, piling onto their big bed or perching ourselves on their armchairs with pieces of the morning paper. It's probably no surprise that I've always been a morning person, getting up at the crack of dawn, getting to work early.

My father wasn't all business, though. He spent a lot of time with his family. He loved tennis and canoeing and entertaining with my mother. And he liked to paint watercolors. I think I may have gotten my artistic nature from him.

I didn't always know I wanted to be a designer, although one of the first ways I made money was sewing custom leather hippie clothing in college. What can I tell you, it was the 1970s. I fell in love with both literature and art while at Brown. Ultimately, art won out, and that led me in the direction of fashion. After I graduated, I took some courses in fashion design at the Rhode Island School of Design, which was just down the street from Brown, and St. Martin's School of Art in London, which was an adventure that gave me a new perspective on my limited experiences at that time.

My year in London was life changing. The St. Martin's course was a total immersion in design. We spent hours at the Victoria and Albert Museum studying Chinese porcelains and African masks and whole days visiting art galleries looking at contemporary art, and we walked miles throughout the year keeping up with the hippest boutiques. I have never sketched so much since that year—nonstop, project after project. I went through reams of paper, boxes of pens, whole packages of colored pencils. It was intense and exciting. The St. Martin's teaching philosophy was that everything visual can become an inspiration for fashion design—art, ballet, street people. After the four years of academic, intellectual life at Brown, this called on completely different senses—visual, aesthetic, tactile. I loved it.

Going abroad really opened my eyes, although it didn't expose me to the variety of learning styles in the world. That education would come later, courtesy of Charlotte.

Two years after graduating from Brown and with some very whimsical, fantastical student sketches in my portfolio, I embarked on a three-week job search.

I pounded the pavement of New York City's Garment Center day after day, ducking between the men pushing wardrobe racks along the sidewalks, from one company to another, before I finally landed a job as a junior designer at a small sportswear company. Once I found work, I was on my way. I found a huge, bohemian loft in Tribeca to live in—with no real bathroom and no buzzer from downstairs—so I felt like a cool, downtown New York chick. I was loving life, working hard, and playing hard, sometimes staying out all night at loft parties or at Tribeca's legendary dive, the Mudd Club.

HAVING IT ALL

One position led to the next, which led to six years working with Liz Claiborne as a knitwear designer. And that ultimately brought me to my own brand. Liz Claiborne and her husband, Art Ortenberg, had decided to add a higher-end label and asked if I would design the collection. They actually asked me if I would be *willing* to put my name on it. Willing? Willing!

This was a Cinderella dream—what every young designer longs for. I had worked hard since I got out of school. The fashion business is cutthroat and difficult to get ahead in, but I just kept at it. In my years working as a knitwear designer for Liz Claiborne, I put in long, long hours, traveled to factories in Asia, sometimes as often as nine times a year. In that time, I got to work closely with Liz. I admired her tremendously, and we became good friends. But I never dreamed that would lead to her and Art offering me my own label. I was over the moon.

I got pregnant shortly after I received the offer. Soon, I would be living out the feminist fantasy from my college days—I'd be a high-powered career woman, but that wouldn't interfere with my being a wife and a mother, too.

So there I was, thirty-five years old, with a new husband, a new company, and a new baby on the way. I was exhilarated. I felt proud, powerful, and optimistic. It would be a long time before I would realize just how difficult some of the aspects of this "having-it-all" lifestyle were. For the moment, I was convinced that I was creating an example for other women to follow.

SHOWTIME

I loved being pregnant. It was a wonderful pregnancy—a little bit of morning sickness the first three months, then nothing. It was an exciting time for Tom and me. We were still in the blush of new romance, and we reveled in our adoration for and support of one another.

I worked until two weeks before Charlotte was born. I wanted and needed to tie up all my loose ends as a knitwear designer for Liz Claiborne so that I would have a clear head for my new label—a challenge we agreed I'd take on when I returned from maternity leave. Beyond logistics, I also felt it was important to let nothing slip—as part of my feminist duty to show that pregnancy needn't interfere with a working woman's ability to do her job. I'd eat two huge lunches at work—one at 11 a.m. and one at 2 p.m. Then, I'd eat an early dinner—again a mountain of food—and be so totally exhausted I'd fall asleep between bites. Literally, I'd find myself nodding off as I was eating. I knew that once the baby was born, I would go back to work. In those days, that wasn't a given. Everyone asked, "Are you going back to work?" It was still a new thing for moms to return to their careers.

As my pregnancy progressed, though, and I finished up my work, I noticed something very interesting—the career piece of the equation became slightly less appealing to me. I wavered. One minute I was jumping for joy about my new label. The next, I was lamenting how tough the fashion business is. I'd been in the business long enough to know it was very competitive. An infinite number of factors determined whether a designer was successful or not, besides drawing beautiful clothes. There were also fit, fabric, quality, shipping on time, and perception of the retailers and customers, to name a few. So many wild cards. Maybe I was just having career anxiety. This would be my most difficult design task to date. It wasn't designing a couple of individual garments, it was creating a whole new label, a collection—determining how dressed up, how casual, how sporty, how refined, what price point, how luxurious. I worried, *What if nobody liked what I designed for the Dana Buchman line?*

At some point before I went back to work, my fears escalated, and I started to have moments of real, sharp anxiety. It was intense. I was "on" twenty-four hours a day. There was so much to be done, so much that was new, that I was doing for the first time. And it all had to be right, it all had to be "fabulous." The rush of adrenaline never left my body. I was on the phone to Asia and Italy in the evening, sketching in the middle of the night, and working on the prototypes and with stylists for the show itself during the day. It was heady, magical, the stuff that dreams are made of. I was never tired because I was so excited. I was anxious and fearful that it wouldn't be good.

I kept these feelings to myself. I realized that if I failed, it would be a very public failure. I'd be letting down Liz and Art, my friends, my mentors, my surrogate parents. I'd be losing money for my fellow employees at Liz Claiborne, as well as the shareholders. How embarrassing. I ran through mental scenarios from hell: *the launch fashion show ends and the audience sits there stock still, horrified at the collection . . .*

BRINGING UP BABY

Long before I didn't know what it was like to have a child with LD, I didn't know what it was like to have a child at all. If you can believe it, all the time I was pregnant and enjoying those pregnancy hormones, I thought very little about what it would be like to have a baby. I was so wrapped up in work, the whirl of thinking about my own collection, of being a newlywed.

Babies were unfamiliar territory. I had only one woman friend in New York City, and she didn't have any children. None of my colleagues and acquaintances at work had babies. I hadn't held many infants in my life up to that point.

All this is to say, I had no idea how much in love with Charlotte I'd be from the minute she arrived. My baby was the most fascinating thing I had ever seen. It was almost comic to me how I'd instantly transformed from being totally indifferent to babies to being totally mesmerized. It must be nature's way of maintaining the species. It was a total, hormonal, undeniable, full-body change in my very being: I just wanted to be with Charlotte. All the time.

It came over me the moment I held her in the delivery room. I had never felt anything like this. It was just like in the movies. I cried at the miracle of birth (that was before the painkiller wore off from my Caesarean, and I began crying from pain). I marveled at the wonder of it all. All of a sudden, I got it; I knew what it was to feel like a mother.

But along with the joy, the pride, the love, I felt a sense of being in the dark. I didn't know how to take care of babies; I didn't know they cried so frequently; I had never experienced diaper rash; I didn't know what supplies I needed; I didn't know when to be worried or when something was not such a big deal, like cradle cap or a crispy umbilical cord drying up and falling off. There was a whole vocabulary and range of experiences I had no knowledge of and was terrified to encounter. Sweaters—ask me anything about sweaters and I can tell you. Babies—not a clue.

In fact, you'd think I hadn't been expecting a baby at all, from how ill prepared I was for Charlotte's actual arrival. When I went to the hospital to deliver her, I brought no clothes to take her home in. And it was a cold October day. So the designer's daughter had to wear a hospital-issue stocking cap, and, luckily, they let us take the blanket she had been using in her hospital crib.

I was truly out of my element. I wasn't prepared for the crying, the waking up several times in the night for feedings, the sleep deprivation. Charlotte was colicky. There were just these long, inexplicable crying jags, and I could do nothing to stop her. It sounds silly, but no one told me about these aspects of having a baby. I felt like I'd missed an important year at school where they covered the topic.

I felt so disappointed that my otherwise beautiful, relaxed, calm, smiling, heavenly infant—this child who filled me with an instant suffusion of love—would turn into a purple-red, tightly wound ball of rage and pain from hell. What was wrong with *me*, I wondered, that I couldn't comfort my child. What was wrong with *her* that my overwhelming love couldn't comfort her?

I managed, as always, to keep a cool exterior. But, internally, I was losing my calm. What internal misery was making that little body convulse in distress? I'd get tired. Empathy would fade, replaced by despair, and, then, anger would begin to well up inside. Anger was the emotion I couldn't stand, the emotion I was never supposed to have, let alone exhibit. I'd just hold it in and struggle with my frustration over having no idea how to handle this.

Eventually, this unease, this not knowing, abated as far as the day-to-day care went. But it was to return when Charlotte's rate of development became a serious issue at age three. It's been part of my life ever since.

BACK TO WORK

Charlotte was born in October. Two months later, in December, I went back to work to launch my new label. That was one of the hardest things I have ever had to do. Of course, I was excited about my new company, but my grief at leaving my baby each day was all encompassing.

That March, when Charlotte was five months old, I had to take a nine-day trip to Italy to shop for fabrics for my collection. I'll never forget how hard it was for me to get on that plane. It was an undeniable career demand, but aside from the pain of leaving Charlotte, I had another problem: I was still nursing.

When breastfeeding, I felt like an archetypal, mythical good mother. Charlotte had needs, and I could fulfill them—the opposite of the feelings evoked by her colic. Women in prehistoric times had done this, as had the ancient Greeks, the Romans, my grandmothers. I was joined with the mothers of all ages.

In order to keep the milk going, I had to pump while in Italy. I went out and bought a portable plastic pump. I will never forget the first night, in the bathroom of the fantastic Excelsior Hotel in Florence, trying to pump. I couldn't work the darn thing. It kept falling apart into the sink. Here I was, in one of the most beautiful, old luxury hotels in the world, surrounded by magnificent furnishings, marble, heavy drapes, and majestic high ceilings, and all I felt was grief and inadequacy and loneliness. I wasn't with my baby or my sweet husband. I was way over there in Italy, and I couldn't even work the breast pump.

I recall sobbing into the marble sink. The period of breast-feeding was officially over. I felt deeply sad and alone. And I had an inkling that my big career was going to exact a heavy price.

IT TAKES A VILLAGE

As soon as I got pregnant, Tom and I knew that we would need full-time, live-in help. The demands of my work were huge. In addition to my full-time office hours, I needed to travel several times a year to yarn shows in Florence, fabric shows in Paris, factories in Asia. I needed the flexibility to be able to go into work early or to stay late with little notice. Tom had taken three months off between jobs in law firms when Charlotte was born, and he'd be going back to an even more demanding job than the one he'd left. We needed a live-in nanny.

Although I knew that this was necessary, I felt a little funny about it. There would be a stranger living with us. And she would spend more time with my child than I would. I wondered if Charlotte would identify with this new, strange person as her mother rather than me. I was also self-conscious that it might seem like some extravagant indulgence. Would the nanny see me as spoiled? Would other people? But really, there was no other way to juggle my job and motherhood.

Tom put an ad in the *Irish Echo*, a small weekly newspaper catering to the Irish community in New York. We found a lovely young Irish woman who was just moving to New York. She came to live with us when Charlotte was just a month old. But she didn't last long—she went home to Ireland for Christmas and didn't come back.

We went back to the *Irish Echo*, and it led us to Monica Lowe, a lovely Jamaican woman who is still very much involved with helping us take care of Charlotte and her younger sister, Annie, and with helping to manage Charlotte's LD.

I learned so much from Monica from the very beginning. She was a mentor to me in the world of childrearing. I mentored young designers at work, and she mentored me at home. She was totally relaxed. She wasn't afraid of breaking Charlotte. She wasn't afraid of her crying, her colic. Her whole body language was relaxed. She laughed easily. I felt totally confident that she would look after Charlotte with all the care I would—but with a lot more knowledge.

That's not to say it was always easy. The qualities I admired in Monica—her strength, her conviction—sometimes caused me unease. Some of her island habits didn't jibe with mine. Some of her potions for common ailments were "folk" remedies I was unfamiliar with. Of course, in the New Age 1990s, I learned that many of them were not only effective but were beginning to be accepted by even some mainstream doctors—hot garlic and cayenne-pepper tea really does relieve the discomfort of cold symptoms! At the time, that home-concocted medicine scared me more than some totally chemical potion from the pharmacy.

But Monica was a natural where child rearing and healing were concerned. We had a three-foot-long section on the bookshelves of childcare how-to and reference books. Monica had her experience and her instinct.

Monica was—and still is—an essential part of our family unit. I don't know how the family would have functioned without her. We were blessed, right from the beginning. Once we had Monica living with us and helping with the more difficult aspects of taking care of our baby, I could really enjoy Charlotte. We were symbiotic in a way that mothers and their children have been for all time.

I have photos of Charlotte napping on my stomach as I napped. All of the maternal instincts I once feared I lacked were now kicking in. I instantly welled up with love and warmth whenever I saw her. She was soft and warm and beautiful. I loved walking around with her in her Snuggly—that harness that straps a baby to your stomach and that is essential to urban living and very primal, kangaroolike, in a wonderful way.

I also loved walking next to Tom as he carried her in the Snuggly. We were the closest we'd ever been then. He'd been home for three months, helping take care of Charlotte, and that was a great, bonding experience for all of us.

Still, even with all that Monica showed us, we knew so little about having a child. We joined a parenting class held by our pediatrician in the West Village. Career moms and dads just like us would show up after work to listen to Dr. Tsao talk about what it would be like to be a parent, from a medical angle. I remember arriving there, still buzzing from goings-on at work—deadlines, plans for a show, hiring, designing—and having to switch my focus to less tangible issues.

It was interesting to be hearing tips from a doctor about what to look out for as far as illnesses and milestones. She told us when our daughter should crawl, when she should walk. I was grateful to have that.

But none of it really registered then. It was academic, just a bunch of facts at that point. Like taking notes in health class in junior high. Charlotte was so young, most of what we were learning wasn't relevant yet.

A few months later, though, when Charlotte didn't crawl on time, it would all come into sharp focus. Suddenly, we would be aware of all sorts of milestones. And everything would change dramatically.

Chapter 2

AT FIRST YOU CRAWL

FIRST-TIME PARENTS ARE A NEUROTIC BUNCH, MAKING note of every little breath their little ones take and agonizing over every development that doesn't happen at the exact moment that Dr. Spock says it should. I was no exception.

When Charlotte was born, it was as if I had landed in another world, and I was more than a little disoriented. In a very short time, I had gone from hard-working and hard-partying single chick in a raw Tribeca loft to married brand-name designer and first-time mom—in a more finished, and bigger, Tribeca loft, which I initially resisted moving to.

We had been living in the fairly roomy, thousand-square-foot space that I had rented since I first moved to New York City, way before Tribeca was chic (and before they called it Tribeca for "triangle below Canal"). It was a corner apartment on the fifth floor of what was once a cold storage warehouse, a quirky place with just one huge room and windows along both outer walls. The rent was cheap, but the apartment wasn't exactly child friendly. It had a really old freight elevator you operated by pulling a rope that wasn't terribly reliable, so we often had to climb the five flights when the elevator was out—imagine doing that with a baby and a stroller, or asking a nanny to do that. There was also no intercom and no buzzer to let people in. Visitors had to yell up to us from the street; we'd throw the key out the window to them in a sock.

Still, I didn't want to move. I had grown attached to the place since I'd been there for ten years and had put so much into it. I had laid the floors myself, and friends of mine built the bathroom—there was none when I moved in, if you can believe that. I didn't want to let go of the Bohemian, downtown loft living I had become so accustomed to and that felt like such a part of me. In the midst of all the other huge changes I was going through, it seemed as if leaving my loft would trigger an identity crisis.

Fortunately, just before Charlotte was born, we found another, much bigger loft just two blocks north of the other one. It was also in gritty Tribeca and had a rusted front door, lots of graffiti, and a working loading dock. Whew—still unconventional. I could go on feeling like myself and right at home. Even better, it was four times the size of the other place and had actual rooms, including one that had, coincidentally, been a nursery for another baby named Charlotte.

AT FIRST YOU CRAWL

As Charlotte began to grow, we started to look out for the milestones we'd read about in books and heard about at the doctor's office. The first one on the list was holding her head up by herself. Check. Then there was rolling over, followed by sitting up. Check. Check. She met all of those right on time. We were amazed and thrilled.

Next, at the six-month mark, we started looking for signs of crawling. Charlotte was six months old in April 1987, and I remember that time especially well because it was when I launched my first collection. There was an evening fashion show with models, music, lights, and my clothes. I was surrounded by family—my mother, sister, brother, and their families had all flown in from Tennessee for this, and Tom and his family were there, too. The show went really well, and I was thrilled. It wound up on the front page of USA Today. Heady stuff.

Back home, though, Charlotte wasn't crawling. Knowing that most babies begin to crawl between six and ten months, we gave it a little more time.

Ten months in, she still wasn't crawling. *Hmmm*, we thought. Still, all the books and Dr. Tsao said that each child is unique and that some kids reach certain milestones at different points.

We did our best not to panic, at least not in any outwardly detectable way. I know that internally, Tom and I were each beginning to worry, but neither of us wanted to let on what we were thinking and feeling. We were so afraid of anything being wrong and of showing each other our fears. It's a shame because we could have helped each other out and become closer instead of beginning to draw apart, ever so slightly.

Eventually, we couldn't avoid talking about it. I remember sitting in Central Park one magnificent sunny afternoon with Tom and his mother, Jackie, when the topic of Charlotte's not crawling yet came up. One of us—I can't remember who—said,

"Shouldn't she be crawling by now?" Another of us even uttered the unspeakable: "Do you think there's something wrong?"

That day was the first time I allowed myself to think that Charlotte might be different in some way. Remember, I had no one to compare her to, no infants in my past, no prior first-hand experience with babies crawling at the right time or the wrong time. I remember feeling almost a searing pain when I allowed the thought to enter my mind. It was like a physical jolt passing through my body. It started with a tingling in my neck and then went inside and through my heart and stomach—a visceral "Oh, no!" feeling, combined with a sense of dread. When I think about it now, I can actually feel the twinge of anxiety, the slight tightening in my chest, the hairs rising on my neck as they did that day.

Those sensations didn't last very long; someone jumped in and said, "Oh, I'm sure she's all right," and we all quickly agreed, conspiring to suppress our collective doubts and fears. We changed the subject, but that didn't make the concern—or the cause for concern—go away. Now, after the oblivion and pride of pregnancy and the purely visceral feelings of taking care of a newborn, the business of comparing our child to a norm, and feelings of uncertainty, crept into our lives.

As it turned out, Charlotte never crawled. Much later on, after she was walking, I heard somewhere that not crawling can sometimes be related to LD. Even if I had known that earlier on, there would have been nothing I could have done about it. I do recall occasionally trying some exercises with her. She'd be lying on her stomach, and I'd move her legs back and forth, as if she were crawling. It was fun, but it didn't yield crawling.

There were some other small clues that something wasn't quite right with Charlotte at that age. We noticed something unusual about the way she moved, especially the way she moved her arms. Her joints seemed especially loose. When I would jiggle her legs and arms, it seemed that her limbs moved very easily, too easily, as if she were made of wet noodles. There was little resistance to my touch. I couldn't help but wonder whether there were enough ligaments in her joints to support her body weight.

WALKING ON

As the time for crawling passed, the time for walking came upon us. Charlotte started to "cruise," standing up by grabbing on to furniture and moving along it while holding on. We stored her little plastic books along a low bookcase, and her favorite activity became pulling herself up, sweeping the books off the bookcase onto the floor, and then turning around to see our reaction. Tom and I would sit after work and watch her do that again and again, laughing and laughing. I think we were quietly relieved by her independence and mobility, each of us privately harboring questions as to whether Charlotte's development was proceeding normally. So, even though sweeping the books off the shelf meant we had to keep picking them up, we were delighted at the mess.

But she was a year old, and she wasn't walking. At fifteen months, she still wasn't. Tom and I could avoid talking about Charlotte's never crawling and slowness to walk for only so long. It started out as a casual conversation:

"Do you think there's anything wrong?"

"I don't know, do you?"

"What could it be if there is?"

"I don't know, I wonder whom we'd ask?"

We would take turns, each alternately playing the roles of the worried partner and the reassuring one. It became a natural, almost involuntary dance between us, which offered a certain amount of relief. Whichever of us was feeling worried brought it up to the other in order to get an opinion—or, more likely, the other's reassurance that nothing seemed wrong. Of course, neither of us had any base of knowledge for an opinion either way. Not knowing felt strange to us both. For your career, you get training—Tom knew about the law, and I knew how to make clothes. But when it came to early childhood development, we didn't know very much at all. All we could do was take turns assuring each other, and wait and see. Even if we had no idea what we were talking about, it was comforting to have a partner to lean on and discuss things with.

As time went on, though, that little routine offered less and less comfort. I tried to be optimistic, thinking, *Charlotte is probably just fine, and if she isn't, we'll eventually find out what is wrong with her, and deal with it. Things are going to be okay.* But then twinges of doubt would creep in. At those times, I'd turn to Tom for companionship in my worry, and tap into his reservoir of *things are going to be all right*. That would alleviate my anxiety briefly. Then, I'd suddenly get a terrifying mental glimpse of Charlotte's having something wrong. I'd promptly slam the door on those thoughts firmly shut.

Then, at eighteen months, Charlotte finally walked. Although that was half a year beyond the one-year-old mark all the books identified as the time to walk, Tom and I were thrilled to be able to laugh at all our worrying of the prior six months and say, "See—everything is all right."

Of course, there was more to worry about. According to the Milestone Police, Charlotte should have been talking by eighteen months as well. She had uttered her first word on time (I was a tiny bit disappointed that her first was "da da," but Tom deserved it). But, then, she didn't broaden her vocabulary beyond that for what seemed like ages.

There would be more and more milestones to watch and wonder about. I will always remember Charlotte's toddlerhood as the beginning of the stage of not knowing. It's a stage that, nineteen years later, still hasn't come to an end and probably never will.

AND THEN THERE WERE TWO

When Charlotte was a little over a year old, I became pregnant with our second daughter, Annie Rose. My pregnancy with Annie was as delightful as my pregnancy with Charlotte had been. I still worked like a crazy person—full steam ahead at work, full steam ahead with Charlotte when I came home. It wasn't easy to stop me, even with a belly full of baby.

My life was changing dramatically, once again. This time around, I was more aware that a new baby would bring radical changes than I had been in my oblivious days expecting Charlotte. Even before Annie was born, I got a sense of the added work of having a second child. I remember that towards the end, right before I delivered Annie, I was immense. One evening after work, I took a walk to the grocery store a couple of blocks away from our apartment with a newly mobile Charlotte, holding her hand. On the way there, I was feeling maternal, peaceful, calm. There I was, with my two babies, one inside, one outside. I bought the few things I had needed and started back. But I had overestimated my walking abilities in my ninth month. The thirty-five extra pounds of baby and fluid felt like they were sitting right on my lower back. Plus, I was carrying the groceries and helping Charlotte. The wind had picked up, and it was dark. I thought, *I can't take another step. I can't make it back to the loft. It's only three more city blocks, but my back hurts, my immense stomach hurts, this bag is heavy.* Then, something came over me. I thought, *I can't be feeling this. I have to walk the rest of the way. There's no one to pick me up. Just one step at a time. I can do it. I can get Charlotte home. People have put up with worse. I have no choice.* This was before cell phones, mind you, so I couldn't just call Monica or Tom and ask them to come help me out by taking Charlotte and the groceries.

At that moment, Charlotte started to whimper. I heard the first peep and knew what was coming. And sure enough, the whimper became a whine and then a wail. She was tired; she wanted me to carry her, to pick her up. She was as convinced that she couldn't walk another step as I had been just a moment before. I picked her up walked two steps and stopped when I felt shooting pain in my lower back. I could not possibly carry Charlotte and the groceries on the outside, and Annie on the inside in my current state of fatigue. I put Charlotte down and started to cry.

Then, I looked around at the dark windswept streets of Tribeca in winter, the tall buildings, the few bundled up people with heads down rushing home to their own lives, and realized that crying was just going to get me colder and more tired. I had this revelation: the mom doesn't get to give up and cry and have someone carry her home, wipe away her tears, and make everything all better. It was a moment of sudden maturity for me. I'd signed on for this, and I had to deal. We made it home somehow. I'd like to think that I put the groceries down and got my baby home without them, but I think that probably, stubbornly, I didn't want to not accomplish the task I'd set out to do.

Annie was born when Charlotte was two. We had spent a lot of time telling Charlotte about the baby coming, that she'd have a little sister. She seemed totally fine with that information.

When I went in for my Caesarean, Charlotte wasn't allowed to visit for a couple of days. Being away from her for that long was terrible, though I was certainly tied up with baby Annie.

I was fascinated with Annie, not only because that's what happens when you give birth to a child, but because she was so different from Charlotte—from the very first day. I don't know where I got this idea, but for some reason, I had thought that all infants were pretty much the same. But there, in the hospital, I could see at once that Annie was totally unlike Charlotte. She moved differently. She was stronger, and she didn't sleep at all the first night, not a wink. She just wiggled and squirmed. I remember wishing the nurse would come take her away so I could sleep and then feeling horribly guilty at such an unmotherly desire.

When Charlotte came to visit me, I was ecstatic to see her. She came into the room and lit up when she saw me — it was that total adoration and joy that mothers thrive on. Annie was in the hospital nursery at the time, so I was able to hug Charlotte to my heart's content. We then walked down the hall to the nursery. Charlotte actually skipped, she was so happy to see me. I went into the nursery and held Annie up so Charlotte could look through the window at her new little sister. Charlotte's face instantly collapsed. She looked at me, then at the baby I was holding, and then back at me. Such disappointment and grief. Now she'd have to share. This would become an ongoing issue, as it is with most siblings. But in this case, it would later be amplified by Charlotte's learning differences and all the attention they demanded—and took away from Annie.

When I brought Annie home, my world was shaken to the core. I found having two children to be exponentially more demanding than having just one child. For me, it was more like having five children! I got no sleep. Charlotte was still waking up in the night in need of comforting. Annie, of course, woke up to be fed. Sometimes Tom and I would get up four times in one night. And still we were both working fulltime. Of course, I know that lots of people work and raise kids. I don't think anyone would say it's easy. And it's truly astounding that parents can get by on such poor-quality, interrupted sleep.

During the day, it was equally unrestful. I brought Annie home on a Sunday. That Monday, Monica came in, and then the other neighborhood nannies started to arrive with their charges. I remember sitting in the front part of the loft, holding Annie in my lap and holding Charlotte's hand, surrounded by about five neighborhood nanny/child groupings who had come to welcome the baby. It was loud, chaotic, overwhelming.

I decided to go back to work the next day.

I'd bring Annie into work with me in the morning, all swaddled and asleep, lay her on the design table where she'd continue to nap for a while, then nurse her at my desk or during the fittings after she woke up. In the room where the samples were made, there were sewers and patternmakers from all over the world: Uruguay, Sicily, Russia, Colombia, Taiwan. It was a very family-oriented environment. The men and women welcomed the new addition to our workplace, raving about the beauty of my children. They didn't bat an eyelash when I nursed right in front of them, during fittings, when we would adjust the clothes to a fit model. Tom and I hired a niece of Monica's to come to work with me and take care of Annie when I was in meetings or otherwise occupied. I felt blessed that I had my family at work and my family at home, that I was able to integrate work and children so seamlessly.

Even though I had it all worked out so well, I can admit now that it was a difficult time. I certainly couldn't admit it then. I had everything—full-time, fabulous help; health insurance; enough money; a loving, supportive husband; a dream job; a home within fifteen minutes of the office; two beautiful healthy children. I would have seemed ungrateful if I had spoken up about how hard it was, how I never stopped running.

It was during those years that I learned to just pull myself together and throw myself into the tasks at hand, without paying much attention to my emotions and my needs. I got very little sleep. I was traveling the world for business and working like a maniac when I was in New York. I started to wake up in the wee hours of the morning to call Hong Kong, where some of my clothing was being manufactured. Or I'd go to my drawing table before the sun rose to get some sketching done before the responsibilities of the day erased any creative inspiration that was flowing.

It was exhausting. I had absolutely no time to relax by myself, to read for hours as I had always loved to do. I imagine Tom felt he had much less time for himself. And there was a lot less time available for the two of us as a couple. Having children was like having a TV on all the time—it sucked up all our attention. Our relationship became more and more heavily focused on our babies. It was a foreshadowing of what was to come as Charlotte's LD took on a life of its own, with scheduling needs and with its enormous but hidden impact upon the family as a whole.

COMPARE AND CONTRAST

Now that Annie was born, I had someone to compare Charlotte to. I realized immediately that they were two different human beings, that they were individuals, and that they were who they were from the second they were born. Comparing siblings has been part of humanity since Cain and Abel. But, as we began realizing that Charlotte's development was different from the norm, comparing Charlotte and Annie took on a whole other resonance in our family.

All the time that we had been wondering whether there was something delayed in Charlotte's development, whether there was something wrong with her, my mother and my in-laws were all very supportive. They would listen to our concerns with love and attention. None of them had had any first-hand experience with LD or with childhood-development issues, so they couldn't give us specific advice. But, eventually, Tom's parents gently recommended checking Charlotte out with a doctor. It was nice how calm they all were about it—not at all alarmist. There was not a meddler or a know-it-all among them. They kept telling us how beautiful and adorable Charlotte was and how much they loved her and us.

Later, when she was about three and in preschool at a Montessori school called Washington Market, Tom and I really started to observe things. Charlotte's speech wasn't clear. The individual words weren't enunciated and were hard to understand. She didn't speak in complete sentences, and she'd tell stories out of sequence—she'd start in the middle or at the end and wouldn't understand why we couldn't follow. She also had trouble counting; she couldn't tell you whether there were three or four marbles right in front of her on the table. We also noticed that Annie reached several developmental milestones much earlier than Charlotte had—crawling, walking, speaking.

FACING REALITY

We have a videotape of Charlotte from that year that is very telling. It was taken during a spring festival in a park in downtown Manhattan right next to the school. It was a beautiful morning, filled with the hopeful scent of leaves budding on the trees. Charlotte's class had learned a dance, and they were going to perform it for all the park to see. They all marched out of the school to where the parents were assembled. The music started over the loudspeaker, and the whole line of children started moving to the music. Charlotte, obviously enjoying herself, excitedly started moving as well, laughing and swaying and cavorting full force—*in the opposite direction.* When she realized that she had gone right and the rest of the kids had gone left, she paused for a moment, laughed, shrugged, and then kept dancing—except to the right now and much less certainly this time.

We took a lot of videos in those days, usually on Sunday mornings, and there's more to them than merely lasting documentation of Charlotte's LD. It would be the four of us in the loft. The place looked as if a bomb had hit it, with clothes, toys, and dishes strewn everywhere. Tom mostly worked the camera. He'd train it for long stretches of time on the girls playing dress-up; little Annie perched precariously on a stool, pulling clothes out of a cabinet and then throwing them on the floor. You can see me in those videos, padding around barefoot, totally calm and happy with my sweet family during what precious little time we had just to relax together. I love to go back and look at the footage of our happy, easy time because it reminds me that it hasn't all been a struggle. Still, as I rewatch those tapes, witnessing Charlotte's awkward movements, I am reminded of how difficult it eventually became to rationalize her apparent differences away.

At a certain point, it became fairly obvious to us that something wasn't right, but the school disagreed with us, which frustrated Tom. The Montessori philosophy is that kids naturally develop at different rates and eventually end up where they want to be. There seemed to be some merit to this philosophy—indeed, we agreed, in theory, which is why we'd picked the school in the first place. We wondered whether it was unrealistic to expect our daughter to achieve certain things at particular, prescribed times. As first-time parents, we really didn't know how much attention to pay to those prescribed times. Legend has it, after all, that Einstein didn't talk until he was five years old! I don't like to come off as pushy, so when the supposed experts at the school said everything was all right, I thought we should listen to them. Even though I was concerned, I tried to convince myself that everything would take its course in time. I'm from the South, from a family that didn't seek out the care of doctors much. Tom, on the other hand, was less acquiescent; he convinced the school to have its psychologist do an evaluation. The results showed nothing unusual in Charlotte's development.

Fortunately, Tom wasn't convinced and looked further for clues. He asked our dentist to examine Charlotte's mouth to see whether there was anything physically preventing her from speaking clearly. The dentist couldn't find anything, but she suggested we take her to a speech therapist who could tell us if something else was going on.

Enter Leda Molly, M.S., CCC, SLP/A, a speech therapist and a most important figure in our LD journey. Leda didn't just diagnose Charlotte's language deficits and work with her on them for thirteen years; she also helped us to find many other key professionals who could evaluate and help Charlotte in other ways. Leda became our guiding light through the vortex of new information and hurdles we faced as the parents of a child with learning differences.

Charlotte would ultimately come to be diagnosed with dyslexia, attention deficit disorder (ADD), and a host of other challenges that were incredibly confusing to us. She would not only require speech therapy but would also need special attention to learn how to read and do math, would have difficulty with directions and physical orientation, not to mention motor skills, and would always be confounded by numbers.

While at nineteen Charlotte still grapples with most of these issues, with great determination she's learned to compensate for and cope with them. I once thought her problems were the end of the world, and I doubted seriously whether she would be able to live independently some day. Now, I see not only that Charlotte can live a happy life on her own but that she has gained perspectives and possesses strong emotional instincts that could lead her to be happier even than some people who face fewer difficulties.

But back then, even with Leda's guidance, it was the beginning of a most confusing time for us. Charlotte would endure test after test, and the more information we got back, the less we would understand. It was like quicksand.

Chapter 3

TESTING, TESTING

IT'S NOT EASY TO ACCEPT THE POSSIBILITY THAT THERE might be something not quite "normal" about your child. It's a blow to a parent's ego. It also brings up feelings of guilt, with thoughts like, *Could this be my fault?*

A great way to avoid accepting such a possibility is not to find out—to stay in denial.

But early on, we were encouraged not to deny what was going on: Leda recommended a neurological evaluation. She had observed that Charlotte had difficulty concentrating, in addition to an articulation deficit and difficulty with expressive language.

Tom and I had also noticed that Charlotte had difficulty relating a story in sequence, didn't always understand what she was told, and sometimes spoke in ways that were very hard for us to understand. That seemed unusual to us for a four-year-old. Not to mention that Annie, at two years old, was having less trouble with these things. Also, Charlotte couldn't count. If you put three marbles on the table, she couldn't tell you how many were there. Most kids can count before they're four. And when we played board games with her, like Candy Land, she didn't seem to be able to match up her counting with the way she moved her pieces along the board. We knew Leda was right.

EVALUATION TIME

When Leda suggested that we get Charlotte tested, I was oddly elated. I had been fighting feelings of sadness prior to that, struggling to keep out the possibility of Charlotte's issues. All my life, I had thought most difficulties were solvable. If something was difficult for me, all I had to do was apply myself and work hard, and it would all work out. Suddenly, here was this thing I had no control over.

If Charlotte could be tested, my thinking went, then there must be a concrete thing to test for and then a remedy or course of action. It can be very seductive to submit your child to a battery of tests, hoping that it will yield a printout detailing every capability and deficiency of his or her brain. You think you're going to be handed a clear-cut diagnosis, along with a prescription and a prognosis, and that's the end of the problem. In my experience growing up, you went to the doctor, the doctor gave you some medicine, and you were done.

I felt excited. I was relieved and happy and felt like I was in control again. I would soon know what Charlotte "had," how severe it was, and what I had to do. A test, a doctor, a diagnosis. A rational plan of action. The end to not knowing. I liked that!

Once we made up our minds to get Charlotte evaluated, we decided to go for the big guns. We took her for her first neuropsychological evaluation and testing at Columbia Presbyterian Medical Center, which was said to be the best place for this. There, Charlotte met with a psychologist named Rita Haggerty seven different times over a period of several months.

Columbia Presbyterian was an awe-inspiring place. It's a highly respected institution housed in a huge, imposing building that looms over the Upper West Side of Manhattan. Like most hospitals, it's the kind of place that makes you feel like you should whisper respectfully.

Holding my little four-year-old's hand, it occurred to me how tiny, how fragile, how young she was to be in these intimidating halls. The potential seriousness of her situation hit me as we rode up in the wood-paneled elevator, and even more so in Rita Haggerty's office. Her office was way up high. It had no windows, just dim fluorescent light, nasty industrial carpeting, and green Naugahyde chairs. It was clinical and impersonal. Not an everything's-going-to-be-all-right kind of place.

At the same time, I felt excited and expectant: the very majesty of the hospital that had inspired awe in me also instilled confidence in its ability to help me and my little daughter. I was suffused with the fearful, awed, respectful feelings inspired by the best fairy tales—maybe there would be magic at work here.

The experience of being neurologically tested was tiring for Charlotte, but she didn't appear to mind too much. A neurological test isn't like a blood test or a CAT scan—it's not so obviously quantitative or hard science. It's more like a school test, with multiple choice, word meanings, interpretations of stories, interviews, and visual games, all gauged to test a child's mental aptitudes and abilities in different areas. I had not been allowed to sit through those tests with Charlotte, but over the years I've caught glimpses. A lot involve the tester's asking questions and making judgments and evaluations about the child's answer. Some involve movement in an effort to assess coordination. While some of the tests are quite black and white, some rely a lot on the judgment of the evaluator.

But Charlotte had always interacted well with adults and seemed to enjoy that aspect of it. She viewed her tests as sort of a game, and I think she found all the attention gratifying. She didn't think of what she was doing as tests, things she would be graded on, or could fail at—so there was no anxiety on her part. She enjoyed spending time with a grownup who was kind, who didn't speak too fast for her, who sat in little kiddie chairs at her level. And I think she enjoyed having the chance to communicate in her own way.

BUT WHAT DOES IT ALL MEAN?

I eagerly awaited the findings from all the tests. At the end, we were handed four pages of "this is your child," with charts and test scores and evaluations that left me speechless. I read the results. And read them again. And again. There were lots of mysterious, vaguely unsettling findings, some quantitative, some verbal.

Just the names of some of the tests left me dumbfounded:

- Raven's Coloured Progressive Matrices (Come on. But don't you love that name?)

- The "WPPSI-R," which is whimsically called the "Wipsey" but is really the Wechsler Pre-School and Primary Scale of Intelligence—Revised," an IQ test of some sort, I think
- The Merrill-Palmer Scale of Mental Tests

The observations of those who administered and evaluated the tests were even more perplexing. She was believed to have neurological dysfunction with

1. mild hypotonia
2. immaturities of fine and gross motor coordination
3. poor visual processing
4. poor temporal sequential organization for unrelated material, but normal organization for meaningful material
5. variable linguistic functioning
6. attention deficit with distractibility, impulsivity, and hyperactivity (fidgetiness)

The conclusion stated, "In summary, Charlotte has language, fine-motor, and visual-motor integration difficulties. In terms of her cognitive profile, she is at significant risk for learning difficulties."

Finally, what I was looking for—a diagnosis: she was "at risk for learning difficulties." Okay.

Learning difficulties. Now, what did that mean? I was disappointed and bewildered all at once. I wondered if I was stupid, or nuts, because in no way did I feel the relief and sense of "Ah-ha, so that's it!" that I had been expecting to feel. I wondered why someone would be happy with vague test results like these. Why would a place like Columbia Presbyterian Hospital administer a test that came up with no more conclusive findings than this?

Even today, when I reread all of Charlotte's early test results, which I've kept in this huge, ever-expanding folder, I again feel the disappointment and slight depression from that day course through my body. I am again overwhelmed by the memory of that time in our lives, when I had no idea what impact this list of negatives would have on Charlotte's life.

Missing was an explanation that LD is a big, complex umbrella term that covers all sorts of conditions, that it differs widely from person to person and changes as the child grows older. That the tests for LD are not like the tests for strep throat or malaria; rather, LD tests on kids that young help to identify indicators of a child being "at risk" for LD but often don't get more conclusive than that.

I say that this information was all missing. It may be that I was told but, in my surprised and scared state, couldn't hear it. I have blocked out a lot of the specifics of that time. It was the beginning of one of the most painful periods of my life.

FACING THE MUSIC

We talked with Rita after we got the results back. I can't recall the exact details of the conversation with her—I couldn't remember them from the minute I left her office. I've read that this is common when people receive an unfavorable diagnosis, that doctors often recommend having someone there with you to witness the interaction and remember for you.

But I can remember the general scene. Tom and I were sitting in her dim office like parents in a TV drama. When Rita told us that all indicators pointed toward Charlotte's having "learning disabilities," I felt the tears well up. I didn't sob and scream because that's not my way. I'm way too controlled for that. Years (and generations) of control and unrelenting optimism helped me to keep from falling apart right there.

It all happened in one afternoon, one meeting. Maybe one hour. Rita said Charlotte had LD. I had no idea what LD was, really. And Rita didn't know exactly what Charlotte had. Charlotte was too young for them to be able to determine so many things—how LD would affect her reading, her socialization, her ability to live alone. I've since learned that before a child is about five, or of reading age, the brain isn't yet developed enough for tests to indicate these things.

Rita told us that she couldn't say for sure how severe Charlotte's condition was or what it would mean for her as an adult. Here I was, hearing from a doctor who had done extensive tests, quantifiable tests, that Charlotte had *something* but getting no clear explanation of what it was and what impact it would have on her life. I kept asking what it all meant, and Rita kept telling me as best she could. I asked whether Charlotte would be able to go to a regular school. Rita said she didn't really know but added that it was possible she might be better off at a special school. She started to tell us that there were schools just for LD kids, that some kids started out at them and then went on to mainstream schools. When she said "mainstream," I felt this longing, as if a mainstream school, any mainstream school, would be the epitome of what I would want for my child. *Oh, please, let her go to a mainstream school,* I prayed to myself.

That was pretty ironic, considering that prior to this experience, I would only have wanted a fine, academically oriented school for a child of mine, a place that would stimulate her curiosity, challenge her, and bring out what I hoped, assumed, would be her formidable academic intelligence. Now, the less lofty idea of simply mainstream seemed so far removed, so out of reach, and because of that, even more desirable.

HITTING HOME

In that one hour of talking with Rita, I suddenly saw my child, my baby, as not like other kids. Different. *Disabled* is what the diagnosis said. It felt final, and it felt unfair. This was a Doctor with a Diagnosis, so it had to be accurate. She had summed up in a few vague words what Charlotte was, and it wasn't normal.

This was very difficult for me to take in. It was this big, unwieldy, uncertain package of information. But it wasn't just the confusion of the diagnosis that I was having a problem with. It was more the knowledge that my daughter, my beautiful little Charlotte, had something about her that was different and that would add difficulty to her life in as-yet unforeseen ways.

It was as if, all of a sudden, the floodgates opened. I felt inundated, drowned by the feelings I had been denying and putting off for the past couple of years, waiting for more information. I could no longer comfort myself with the possibility that Charlotte didn't have something. My standard MO of basic optimism was unraveling.

Learning disability. That was really hitting at the heart of something I had valued all my life—learning was a discipline that my family, Tom's family, and Tom and I held in high esteem. And here it was compromised for our sweet Charlotte.

I had no idea what any of it meant, really, or what we were in for. I also had no idea that while people with learning differences may struggle in some areas, they may also excel in others—I would learn that later. And I would come to find hope and inspiration in the stories of luminaries like Winston Churchill, Pablo Picasso, even Albert Einstein. These were extraordinarily intelligent people who just happened to have lived with certain cognitive challenges.

When we got out of the office, we called Tom's mother, Jackie, his father, Sam, and my mom. I remembered that Jackie had a good friend, Carla, who was a psychologist specializing in learning issues. Jackie recommended that I meet with Carla, give her Rita's results to look through, and get her read on them. I don't remember what my own mother said long distance from Memphis, but I imagine it was soothing and oriented to empathizing with my grief and assuring me that things would be all right.

A few weeks later, I visited Carla for some insight. She wasn't able to shed much light on what Charlotte actually had, even having read Rita's report. But she brought up the topic of special LD schools. What struck me was how she talked about them as if they were a perfectly respectable option. They were normal, okay to talk about. She wasn't horrified by Charlotte's LD or by the prospect of her attending a special school. Her ease in discussing it all helped me to take my first step toward accepting what was happening with Charlotte. At the time, I had no idea it would take me another twelve years or so really to come to terms with it.

Back home that evening, Charlotte greeted us by running to the elevator and jumping into my arms as usual. I was overtaken by a heightened feeling of love for her, even beyond my usual melting at seeing her smiling face at the end of a workday. But another feeling crept in: fear. Now there was something that I knew but didn't quite understand. I was terrified and hoped I didn't show it. I was also amazed to notice that my perception of her had begun to change, now that I knew. She was still happy, cute, funny, and active, but this was the very beginning of a period during which I would gradually lose sight of Charlotte as a whole being. I would begin to see her as a list of problems — problems that I needed to fix.

Only years later would I come to see those four pages of test results for what they were. They addressed just one very small part of this beautiful, creative, college-bound young woman who has uncanny insight into people, who is incredibly compassionate towards others, and who draws and paints so beautifully.

That is not to discredit the value of those tests. They were a crucial element in getting Charlotte diagnosed and getting her the help she needed. In my highly emotional state, I mistook the tests as a complete snapshot of my daughter, and that's what I thought I wanted. There's no question in my mind that Charlotte *had* all the issues the evaluation listed. But, still, those four pages didn't represent the whole child.

THE GREAT ESCAPE

The turmoil of all of this took a toll on me on the inside. I was heartbroken but didn't want to admit that — not to Tom, not to myself. I know that Tom held his fears and anguish mostly to himself as well. It's not that we didn't talk about LD; we did, a lot. But we talked about it in operational terms, logistic terms. I never said what I was feeling. I never said to Tom, "I'm scared." Looking back, I see that this was a terrible waste of an opportunity to help each other, to build emotional intimacy. Instead, we were building distance. Imagine these two people who love one another so much, at this very important time of their lives, not sharing the details of their fears.

I was overwhelmed by it all. It seemed very serious. I didn't know anything about learning differences, and, foolishly, I was afraid that somehow this was a reflection of my own intelligence and my parenting. This may sound absurd, but I thought, *Did I do this? What did I do wrong?* I've since learned that this is very common among parents of children with LD.

There was just one place for me to run from the ache of it all: work.

You might expect that someone going through such a hard time and so busy with taking her daughter for test after test might let her work slip. But not me. No. Never. I threw myself into work, and there was plenty of it for me to get lost in. Things were happening there at breakneck speed. I had to ship a new group of complex sportswear every month, with a variety of garments in a variety of fabrics from all over the world that would be of high quality and fit perfectly and sell sell sell!

I worked more furiously, more intently than ever. I have always prided myself on my powers of concentration and stamina. I felt I could pack more work into each waking moment, cut back on the sleep a bit, and accomplish everything I needed—plus spend my "free" moments at home researching LD.

I didn't really tell anyone at work what was going on at home. Or maybe I would mention it matter-of-factly, but I would never bring up the emotional roller coaster I felt I was on. I didn't want to take the time to explain everything and articulate these feelings I didn't have a handle on. Besides, we had buttons and skirt lengths to discuss. I was also afraid the other women at work might not be interested. I told myself that the more time I spent on personal matters, the longer I'd have to stay to get my job done. But in truth, I was building work into this fort where home problems couldn't interfere. So, I'd just contain it and keep work matters at work and home matters at home.

Boy, was that demented. As I look back, I realize I was bottling my emotions up, making myself into an automaton, stripping myself of feeling at work, thinking that was admirable and necessary for success in business. This spirited but impersonal approach unfortunately became a signature of working at Dana Buchman. It was like a corporate culture of machisma—who could work harder, stay longer. For the most part, we hired only Type A people like my close colleagues and me. I was surrounding myself with people who were sharp as tacks, fast moving, aggressive, decision makers—people completely unlike Charlotte. Can you believe, at one point, a colleague of mine was overheard telling her assistant, "Don't say good morning to me. I don't have time." Back then, it felt heady, efficient, and thrilling. We were fast-moving. You had to cut to the chase. Nail it! There was no tolerance for imperfection, vulnerability, needs. No room for being human.

MORE TESTING

Those seven meetings at Columbia Presbyterian were just the beginning. Over the years, Charlotte saw more professionals who made more confusing assessments than I can count. They ranged from diagnoses that seemed very serious to quirky things we all have.

On the one hand, we read, "In addition to Charlotte's language difficulties, a good part of her expressive dysfluency appears to be neurologically based and may be related to the hand tremors and mistiming she experiences in fine motor and graphomotor tasks." That one scared me. But this one seemed silly to me: "She found it hard to learn a clapping game, which required her to learn a sequence of three movements, repeat them rhythmically, and say a familiar rhyme simultaneously." I mean, is this a serious deficiency that will affect her life? My whole side of the family has a hard time finding the beat. When a neurologist noted Charlotte's "plantar responses were flexor and there was no ankle clonus . . . dyskinesias on finger opposition and imitative finger movements, incoordination on stressed gait," I wondered, is that medicalese for the problem with the beat?

Until junior high, Charlotte submitted to all of the testing willingly, enjoying the interaction with people who were trained to hear what she was saying, who would let her finish her sentence. Sometimes physical fatigue got to her, though. There were tests she had to take every year to demonstrate to the Board of Education that she still had LD, even though it's incurable. Those tests were given at the other side of town from where we lived, and by the time Charlotte had gotten there on the subway and walked to the office, she could be drained and cranky.

As for me, in spite of that first disappointment with the Columbia Presbyterian tests, I couldn't help but place high expectations on hearing test results. I would let myself get my hopes up, hoping I would learn a little more about what was going on in Charlotte's brain. Until Charlotte's last test, right before her senior year, I always expected them to sum her up and show us the way.

All the LD tests try to quantify what's going on in the mind of the LD kid. They might rate Charlotte's aptitude for something or indicate in what percentile her math skills or language abilities rated, compared to other kids her age. Some of the percentiles were shocking to me. She was just off the charts in some areas, and I don't mean off the tops of the charts. The first time I heard some of these percentiles, I was speechless. For example, in seventh grade, she had the math skills of a third grader. When I read something like that, my blood would run cold. I'd hear an imaginary thud in my mind and think, *Whoa, now what?*

By the end of ninth grade, Charlotte was fed up with all the testing. She was tired of taking that same test for the Board of Education, year after year, for six years. She began complaining about the tests' wasting her time, making her feel ridiculous. It must have been humiliating, having to prove again and again that she needed the help she did.

Charlotte endured her very last set of tests with Dr. Anita Dick, a psychologist, in the summer before her senior year of high school. Dr. Dick had been the psychologist at one of Charlotte's elementary schools, so she had known her for years. She did the final LD testing of Charlotte's life, the one that was required for college, so she could qualify for LD status. That would get her tutoring help, books on tape, and more.

I must say, those were the most worthwhile tests Charlotte ever took. Maybe it had something to do with my not expecting too much. Maybe it had to do with Dr. Dick's using her knowledge of Charlotte to test her in a more holistic way.

Even nicer was the way in which she delivered the results. She didn't just hand us a bunch of charts and numbers. She made time to meet with Tom and me, and then the three of us. She spent several hours talking about Charlotte's whole learning profile—what she was good at, what she was excellent at (I had never heard the word "excellent" in our previous years of testing!), what she had a hard time with, what she was afraid of. We heard not just negatives, but lots of positives as well. We were getting a glimpse, finally, of the whole Charlotte. Unfortunately, this picture of Charlotte as more than the sum of her disabilities was many years away.

Chapter 4

SCHOOL DAZE

ONCE WE HAD HAD CHARLOTTE TESTED, IT WAS TIME
to make decisions about where to send her to school. Sending
your child to school for the first time is a doozy even under the
best of circumstances. Sure, it's a thrilling milestone, but it also
leaves you pining for those early years. For me, sending Charlotte, my first baby, to school was fraught with even more emotion. In addition to facing the fact that she was growing up, I had
to grapple with the notion of sending her to a special school for
kids with learning differences.

After we got the results of her evaluation at Columbia Presbyterian Medical Center, we weighed the options—mainstream
school versus special school—and came to the conclusion that a
special school would be the right place for Charlotte, at least to
start. Who knew? Maybe she'd get enough help there to move
on eventually to a regular school.

It was a very difficult and painful decision to make. A special school, with its much smaller classes, was a foreign concept to me. It wouldn't be anything like my experience at public school in Memphis, where there were lots of kids in each classroom, and the hallways bustled with activity. Truth be told, I think I also felt ashamed. Here I was, an A student all my life, an overachiever, an approval addict, and now I had a child with special needs. What would I tell people when they asked what school my daughter went to? In Manhattan, there's fierce competition even to get into private nursery school programs, let alone prestigious elementary and high schools. Everyone always wants to know where everyone else's kids rank in comparison to theirs.

I've since learned that this initial shame is common for parents of children with learning differences. In fact, many are so freaked out by their children's condition, so uncomfortable with the idea of a special school, that they let their kids struggle in mainstream situations. They want to believe their children will outgrow their difficulties or that "inclusion" in regular classrooms will somehow help them socially, when often it worsens things for them. I've been told that kids with severe LD are often too intimidated to participate in mainstream classrooms. Even more stigmatizing than going to a special school is sitting in a classroom and feeling inadequate compared to the other kids.

Of course, not all kids with LD need to go to special schools— only kids with more severe cases. Also, in many places, there aren't any special schools, so there's no choice other than to send LD kids to mainstream schools, where they're taught in "special ed" classrooms by special teachers. But in New York City, there are several special schools to choose from. And, at first, I didn't want to have to look at any of them.

SHOPPING AROUND

A short time after receiving the results of Charlotte's evaluation, we started researching schools. We consulted with Tom's mother's friend, Carla, as well as with our guru, speech therapist Leda Molly, about which schools to consider. At first, we were looking not just at special schools but at mainstream private schools equipped to support LD students as well. We wondered which would be the best route for Charlotte, and I think that subconsciously we were still holding on to the possibility of being able to drop a well-respected school name when people asked. On the other hand, getting into private school in New York City is a legendarily grueling and competitive process.

Still, I didn't mind the process. Throughout the stage of researching and evaluating schools and filling out applications, I was a bit more at ease. These tasks called on the operational side of my brain, a part of me I have always been at home with and have sought out when my emotions get too unwieldy. We had a list of about eight places, half mainstream and half special LD schools. After reading about them and making some phone calls, we made appointments to visit them and find out what they were really all about.

When it came time for Tom and me to make the actual visits, I became uptight. I didn't really want to open my mind to the idea of a special school any more than I wanted to accept that Charlotte had special needs.

We started our search with a little LD school in Brooklyn. It was a bright, sunny day. I remember checking in with myself, taking a deep breath, and adopting a "here goes" mentality. Keep your mind open, I told myself. Maybe it will be great.

The school was in a Quaker meeting house. It didn't seem at all bad as we walked toward it. But then I realized the school was in the building's basement. The classrooms were tiny and very dark and cramped, with low ceilings. I imagined that on a gray day, the environment would be as bleak as I felt inside.

The school didn't have very many students, just a few kids in each grade. Another downside, I thought at the time. We came to learn that this was true of all LD schools and that it was one of the strongest aspects of such an environment. With fewer kids per teacher, each of the kids got a larger share of much needed attention.

The woman who took us around was perfectly nice, and I later realized that this school was one of the finest LD schools in New York. But because it was our first visit to one, and I was having a very hard time with the idea of Charlotte's needing a special school, I called up in my mind images of the depressing, hopeless schools written about in *Jane Eyre* and *Nicholas Nickelby*. It was an instant no.

As we left the school, Tom and I were both very quiet beside each other on the walkway. Once we started to talk, on the ride home, we each tried to put on a brave face, assuring one another that this situation wasn't so bad. Inside, though, I think we were both feeling low, depressed. I know I was. We were afraid to admit to reacting so strongly and so negatively to what the experts told us were excellent schools, so, once again, we kept our feelings to ourselves.

We just got back on the horse and looked at more schools. We knew we had to find a school that Charlotte could succeed in, and we had only a few choices and not a lot of time.

Next stop was another LD school on the Upper West Side called the Stephen Gaynor School. This one was situated in a townhouse on many levels. The house had been divided into a warren of itsy-bitsy classrooms. We went on a dark, stormy, rainy day, which didn't help matters. That probably explains why there was a smell of wet blue jeans in the cramped class-rooms. The teachers in each classroom seemed earnest enough, but the kids were sitting almost on top of her and were crowded into tiny little desks with not much room to wiggle. I don't know why I was so hung up on this, but there was no sense of spaciousness.

When the bell rang at the end of the day, the school's center stairway was mobbed with kids pushing and scrambling up and down. I got a feeling of disorder and chaos rather than joy. I now realize my impressions were a reflection of what was going on in-side of me; I was projecting my inner state. Years later, Charlotte would attend Stephen Gaynor, and it would be a great experi-ence for her. She would adore it and find lots of joy and warmth there. But on that day, I was in no condition to see what a won-derful place it was.

It was another instant no.

Finally, we visited a school called Gateway. My resistance was still high. To me, the name sounded like that of a drug rehab center. It had a falsely optimistic ring to it, like something out of a Flannery O'Connor story or a Coen brothers movie. But this was the school that Tom's mother's friend Carla had portentously mentioned when she found out that Charlotte had LD. She said, "I have just one word for you: Gateway."

FINDING THE ONE

Maybe it was because of that recommendation. Maybe it was because this was the third LD school we had visited, and I was getting a better sense of what LD schools were like. Maybe it was because the sun was out that day, and that always puts me in a better mood. But when we toured Gateway with a group of other parents I thought, *This is okay.*

Yes, the school was small like the others, and the classrooms were tiny with very few kids to each teacher. There were only six or eight kids to a class, twenty in a grade, and sixty in the whole elementary school. But having now been initiated, I wasn't as shocked by it all as I had been at the beginning. I was beginning to realize that this came with the territory, and it was our new territory.

I was happy to see that there was a big, light, airy, open room where the kids assembled and had lunch. It was very sunny and spacious. I felt I could breathe, and, at this school, Charlotte would be able to also.

Walking around with the other parents on the tour, I remember looking at some of them and wondering how they were dealing inside. Many were well-dressed career women; several were fathers in suits with briefcases; some appeared to be nonworking moms. They were all very quiet on the tour; if they made any comments at all, they whispered them to their spouses. I had never met any parents of LD kids before. I couldn't help but wonder if they were as freaked out inside as I was. Were they depressed about their child's having to go to a special school, or had they made peace with that fact and accepted it? Were they worried about their child's getting into the school?

I was definitely thinking about that. I recall self-consciously trying to look like a parent they would be pleased to accept, following the tour guide respectfully, looking attentive and interested.

At the end of the tour, as Tom and I walked out, we both agreed that this was the place. I began to feel a sense of relief. At least a decision had been made, and I knew how to move on from there.

THE TABLES ARE TURNED

Now we had to focus on getting Charlotte accepted. It's so funny: I went from resisting the whole idea of LD schools, feeling as if they represented some sort of inferiority, to campaigning to get Charlotte into Gateway. I shifted into let's-do-everything-in-our-power-to-get-them-to-pick-us mode. I was charged with a sense of urgency. *Pick us! Pick us! Pick us!* At a base level, this wasn't just about Charlotte's being selected as worthy to attend; it was about Tom and me being chosen as well.

When Tom, Charlotte, and I showed up for our interview appointment, I felt very nervous. It was exactly that ambivalent feeling of dread and hope that I used to feel in fourth grade, hoping to be picked for the kickball team at Miss Hutchison's School for Girls.

I remember taking great care with my choice of clothes that day. It was as if I thought Tom and I were being evaluated as potential students. I wondered if our being a designer and an assistant district attorney would seem chic and exciting to the interviewers. Would these be careers that they would want to add to their parent roster? I went into my perky, empathetic, intelligent, affluent-without-being-obnoxious shtick. Somehow, I got it into my mind that the headmistress was checking out my shoes, and I got the awful feeling that they weren't up to snuff. She had on Chanel-style low heels, and mine were a funkier fashion pump, maybe with a touch of matte gold. Years later, I would become friends with this headmistress and know for sure that she is not the type to have been grading me on my shoes or other attire. That was just my neurotic fantasy.

Of course, none of this stuff mattered at all—certainly not what I was wearing! Unlike many a prestigious Manhattan private school, the LD schools weren't impressed with where you worked, who you knew, or how much money or publicity you could bring to the school. Instead, they were concerned with whether or not they could meet your child's needs. The acceptance process wasn't at all about Tom and me. It was about Charlotte and what each place might be able to do for her.

The interview went well. We were accepted. And we began our journey along the long road to doing some accepting of our own.

I was still having a hard time getting over myself, getting used to the idea of my daughter going to a special school. As I look back at that time, it's amazing to me that my focus was so not on topic. Why was I worried about the lack of windows in the classrooms and how the headmistress liked my shoes? Why could I not see that there was a wealth of terrific schools to choose from, manned by professionals who knew as much about LD as was known at the time? My own anxiety, shame, and confusion were clouding my vision and my sense of equilibrium. I can't believe that I was so off balance, so tilted emotionally. I thought that by choosing one of these schools, I was picking the best of the worst. In many ways, we were picking the best of the best.

THE RIGHT CHOICE

I remember Charlotte's first day of kindergarten at the Gateway School. She was a little bit excited and a little bit scared, but basically looking forward to a new experience. Two of Charlotte's great strengths are her resilience and optimism. She didn't know the school was a special school; we hadn't told her, and wouldn't for several years.

The school was in the Sunday school rooms of a Presbyterian church on the Upper East Side. It was a small, light-filled space. I noticed right away that it felt like a very nurturing environment. On that morning, there was a lot of jabbering and excitement as the kids arrived. Fortunately, there were a lot of teachers, experts in this mysterious phenomenon called LD. They made sure the chaos was controlled, that the ADD kids were guided and kept on topic, and that the new kids were welcomed and made to feel comfortable from the moment they got there.

Any trepidations I had had about a special school were quickly eliminated. I was pleased that Charlotte was in a place where she would be appreciated for who she was and taught in a way that would work for her. It was a school that recognized the individuality of each child there. And while they made sure the children learned society's mandated ABCs, even more importantly, they helped the children to develop self-esteem. The message to the kids was, *You are smart; you are creative; you are fun and desirable. You have to admire and love yourself as much as we at the school admire and love you.*

The atmosphere that morning was dreamlike, from a children's book about the ideal first day of school. Ms. Pulanco, the kindergarten teacher, exuded warmth and caring. She was the first of the brilliantly gifted teachers who knew instinctively how to reach and teach Charlotte and to impart self-esteem and mastery to her and her fellow LD students. With her sweet brown eyes focused right on Charlotte, she spoke to Charlotte in a soft, comforting voice and listened to her patiently. She exuded calm, and like a magician, she calmed the kids around her.

I remember feeling grateful, relieved. Here were people who noticed that Charlotte learned differently, unlike at her preschool. They were not the least bit alarmed, dismayed, or confused by Charlotte's differences. I felt that I had delivered her into the warm, loving, wise care of a group that would take care of her—and help me take care of her. I felt relieved that she was going to be in good hands, with people who knew about her learning differences and weren't horrified, people who had spent their entire careers figuring out how to manage LD and teach children who had it.

HELPING THE PARENTS

It turns out Ms. Pulanco wasn't just a great teacher for the kids. She and the rest of the school's staff were great teachers for us, too. At Gateway, and really at all the LD schools, they realize that parents are freaked out, and the staff goes to great lengths to help them deal. Here I thought I was the only mom of a Gateway student who felt depressed, confused, and scared, to name a few of my bottled-up emotions, but as it turns out, the phenomenon is common enough that the teachers have a whole philosophy about how to deal with parents.

Recently, Ms. Pulanco explained to me that *many* of the parents of kids at Gateway struggle with the fact of their children's learning differences. Also, it's often their first foray into LD education, and they have no idea what it's all about. They're upset, baffled. She said she has to convey information to them about their kids—about the kids' strengths and weaknesses—piecemeal and very gingerly. Otherwise, the parents can't quite take it in. They become upset and don't really hear. Their defenses go up.

At the time that Charlotte started at Gateway, when Ms. Pulanco said to us, "We are here to help you," I think my defenses were way up. I had no idea that I needed help or that Tom might. I knew Tom was as confused and depressed as I was, but we didn't spend a lot of time talking about it. We held each other, coached each other, soothed each other, but we dealt with uncomfortable feelings by trying to make them go away, not by elaborating on and exploring them.

I realize now with great regret that I didn't take advantage of all the resources available to me as a parent at Gateway. I know that other parents—especially those who didn't work—spent more time at the school and, so, got more out of it. I thought the school was there to educate Charlotte. It never crossed my mind to ask if they had advice and tips for me, for us. I didn't know at the time how much I needed educating and how much my family needed it.

THE DAILY GRIND

Charlotte's going to school at Gateway ushered in a new time and a new routine for the family. Prior to that, both girls were attending preschool at Washington Market School, the Montessori nursery school program that was just around the corner from us and that had been pretty easy for us to manage. It didn't really matter much if they were late, and we could walk them there in just a few minutes. Now, in addition to getting three-year-old Annie there, we had to get Charlotte off to school on the Upper East Side, which is pretty far from Tribeca.

Charlotte had to be downstairs, waiting for the school bus by 7 a.m., dressed, with coat zippered, shoes tied, and lunch in hand. Each one of those details was only achieved after lots of pleading, searching, anger, and frustration. The pressure was high because if Charlotte missed the bus, I would have to take her myself and go thirty blocks north of my office.

As it was, those weekday mornings were pretty intense. They were full of rushing—getting the girls dressed, fed, and off to school with lunch; getting Tom and me coffeed, dressed, and off to work; making sure the three pillars of the family (Tom, Monica, and I) all knew where the others would have to be in the afternoon or evening. The mornings would be followed by a long, intense workday for both Tom and me, followed by rushing home to see the girls in the evening and then the long routine of putting them to bed. And let's not forget the in-between and extracurricular stuff: Charlotte's appointments with assorted therapists and other specialists, school meetings, after-school activities, business obligations.

The problem was, Charlotte wasn't yet able to dress herself in a focused way, and she wouldn't be for several years. It was hard for her to gather her things, tie her shoes, put on her coat, and zipper it up. She was so opposite of me in that way, and I just couldn't relate. I can wake up in the morning and get showered and out of the house in twelve minutes. Literally.

Hardest for me was that I wasn't supposed to take charge and do it for her. Grabbing her hand and efficiently dressing her like a doll was a definite, absolute no-no. How many times was I tempted to do this? No, let's be honest: how many times did I just go ahead and do this in the interest of making the bus and getting to work on time?

There were times when, foolishly, out of pure frustration, I would rush her and snap, "Hurry up, Charlotte!" I'd throw up my hands, lose my patience, and tie her shoes and zip the coat myself, getting more and more angry and frustrated the whole time. For me to exhibit anger like that, I had to be pretty annoyed.

Of course, rushing her was about the most insensitive, counterproductive thing I could have done. She was trying so hard, and she was teetering between the sense that she could do it and the defeated notion that she couldn't. The pressure I put on her just made it more difficult for her.

In hindsight, I realize how many times I was just too harsh, and I feel terrible. I cringe when I think of some of my reactions, early on and, sadly, sometimes even today.

This is where I realize that I have had a learning difference. From the time we learned about Charlotte's LD, through her years of school, I was never able to grasp fully what her experience was or to understand how her brain operated. I tried harder and harder through the years. I educated myself in every way I could think of, and I learned a lot along the way, becoming a better parent and ally for her at every turn. It's sad that it's taken me until now, when Charlotte is just off to college and doesn't need me the way she once did. I sometimes wish I could do the school years over again, starting with the early days at Gateway, but this time with all I've learned.

Chapter 5

RACE FOR A CURE

WHILE I'VE ALWAYS LOVED LEARNING, I HAVE TO ADMIT
that after my formal education was complete, I'd naively assumed that life's learning curve would slow down. But after
Charlotte got into school at Gateway, it was time for me to become a student again, a student of LD this time and, more
specifically, of Charlotte's LD. Here was a whole new world I
knew absolutely nothing about. I bought books, found others at
the library, along with articles, and asked lots of questions of all
the teachers and doctors who worked with Charlotte. I hoped
that, in all of that, there would be some key to understanding my
daughter and how her mind worked. But LD alone is a vast subject, and each case is unique. Indeed, one person's LD can vary
greatly from the next person's; the combination of disabilities is
endless. There's no one-size-fits-all diagnosis.

Actually, in those early days, my deepest hope was that all of the volumes I pored over would hold within them a cure. I didn't yet know that there is no cure for learning differences. Even though I was probably told as much by all the experts we consulted, the information didn't sink in. All I could think of was repairing my little girl. I wanted her *fixed*.

In and around my quest, however, I was mostly learning how to parent a child with LD, how to become her ally and her coach. It took a long time, and there were lots of different challenges along the way. I offered a much different kind of support and help to Charlotte when she was in elementary school than I did when she was in high school, partly because she had different needs at different times, but also in great part because I picked up more important clues as I went along. There were clues about LD in general and clues about who Charlotte was beyond her learning differences. It was truly a hands-on learning experience.

THE LEARNING CURVE

I consider us lucky. In New York City, there are several wonderful schools for children with learning differences, whereas in many other parts of the state and the country, there aren't. Wherever you live, most kids with LD go to regular schools. For some, the resources at those schools are enough to help them; for others, it is a lifelong struggle to get both enough attention and the right kind of attention.

Charlotte had a great experience at the first special school we sent her to; she stayed at Gateway for four years. Her teachers were incredibly patient and attentive, and Charlotte loved going there.

When we originally sent her there at age five, a piece of me thought the school was going to help her develop the cognitive skills necessary for her to then move on to a regular, mainstream school. We were told that with a good number of kids, that happens. But it didn't happen with Charlotte.

I didn't understand: if some kids who had LD could be transformed, why couldn't others? Why couldn't Charlotte?

I didn't know that none of those kids who had moved on to mainstream schools had been transformed, or repaired, so to speak. Their LD hadn't been eliminated. LD can never be eliminated. But it can be remediated and compensated for.

Here's how it works. Learning differences have nothing to do with a lack of intelligence. They are simply the result of different neurological wiring in the brain. Charlotte, despite all her difficulty learning, is quite intelligent—a concept that I didn't get for a long time, and which, unfortunately, a lot of other people don't get either.

With the right kind of help, sometimes the brain's wiring can be adjusted a bit. I see it like this: in the same way that an adult who has suffered a stroke can be retaught to speak, children with visual-processing or language deficits can develop other parts of their brains to compensate for their difficulties. It's a matter of connecting things that were not connected before, of their using different synapses from those that most people use. The result is that they start catching on. The brain circuits have been redirected in a way that helps them process information they couldn't process before. With some kids with less severe cases of LD, that redirecting is more easily achieved and more effective. Those are probably the kind of kids who moved from Gateway to regular schools. Charlotte's case is more complicated and severe.

Where remediation doesn't work, people can find ways to compensate. While remediation helps you get to a higher level, compensation helps you get around the problem. For example, if you want to bring your reading level up from a third- to a sixth-grade level, there are programs designed to teach dyslexic kids like Charlotte different ways to learn to read. Now, say, you want to go to a much higher level and read real literature—you want to read Joyce or Tolstoy. Getting a recording of a book through Recording for the Blind and Dyslexic would be compensating.

SOME FROM COLUMN A, SOME FROM COLUMN B

For many kids, managing LD entails a combination of remediation and compensation. Charlotte needed a lot of both. Finding the right balance of each has been a long pursuit—it's been fifteen years since her diagnosis and counting.

When she was seven, she was mortified to realize that her five-year-old sister could read very well while she hardly read at all. Annie was plowing through Frog and Toad books, and they were out of Charlotte's league. She felt humiliated and pleaded with us to help her. That may have been the first time that Charlotte realized she was different, at least from Annie. We hadn't yet explained to her that she had learning differences—that wouldn't happen for another two years.

About the time that Charlotte started to compare herself to fast-learning Annie, we learned about something called the Lindamood-Bell reading program, a method of teaching kids with dyslexia and other receptive and expressive language disorders how to read. Charlotte is so dyslexic that it is as easy for her to write upside down and backwards as it is to write straight forward. She had problems comprehending what little she could read, and she had serious issues with her speech. The Lindamood-Bell program takes a unique approach to reintroducing kids to the phonetics of reading. There's an emphasis on the relationship between letters, the sounds they make, and the way the mouth moves to make those sounds.

It sounded extremely promising, and we wanted to find out if it could help Charlotte. Alas, it was only offered in California at the time. Still, we knew from talks with Charlotte's speech therapist, who had been the one to turn us on to the program in the first place, that this program might help Charlotte dramatically. It was important—so important that Tom took a leave of absence from work. He put his job on hold so that he could take Charlotte out to the West Coast for this intense remedial reading course. It was a fantastic experience for both of them on many levels. First off, the program worked. Charlotte got the help she needed and cracked the reading code. She also got to have her father's attention all to herself for several weeks! And Tom got to bask in being her knight in shining armor. It was such a success that Tom took time off again the next summer so that he and Charlotte could return. That session helped even more. Charlotte was thrilled, and, of course, we were thrilled for her: at the age of nine, she was now able to read.

Today, she loves to read and often has a few books going at once, although she reads slowly. Still, when books are particularly difficult, she'll get the tape and the book, and use the two together. I am sure that throughout her college career, she will take advantage of the tapes to help her manage all of the reading she'll have to do.

When Charlotte was nine, we tried another form of compensation for some of her issues: medication. For kids with attention deficit disorder (ADD) and attention deficit hyperactivity disorder (ADHD), we were advised that taking medication is a way to get around the problem. When Charlotte was at Gateway, her teachers observed that she was distractible, fidgety, and had difficulty concentrating. The school's occupational therapist evaluated her and discovered she had a problem organizing herself and recommended an evaluation to see whether she had ADD or ADHD. We took her for a neurodevelopmental and neurobehavioral assessment, and it was determined that on top of everything else, she did indeed have ADD.

That "discovery" led to a series of experiments with some very unpleasant pharmaceuticals for about six months. I had read and heard that prescription drugs work beautifully for some kids and adults with ADD, and, so, we had hope. Charlotte went through Ritalin, Cylert, and Adderall. None of them helped her focus or concentrate. They either did nothing at all or made her feel really bad. Some of the drugs brought on depression as soon as they wore off, bringing her to tears for hours, into the night. I can't remember in which order she tried the drugs, or which side effects were associated with which ones. The first was neither good nor bad. So we tried another. For several days, Charlotte would come home from school her normal self. We anxiously watched for signs of clear focus and brilliant attention paying. I imagined I saw marked improvement in the first few days. But then, every day or two, she would come home mopey, with her head down, without energy. The next day, she'd be fine again. It was a "blind" test, so we hadn't told the school she was on drugs. But after a couple of weeks, I couldn't stand not knowing. So, I asked her homeroom teacher how Charlotte had been that week. Ms. Mahoney said, "Now that you mention it, not so good. She has broken down in tears around lunchtime several days in the past week! It's like she was a different person." I told Ms. Mahoney about Charlotte's trying the drug and asked if she had seen any improvement in her performance or focus. The answer was a disappointing no. Even though we were supposed to keep her on the drug for maybe a month or six weeks, it was an easy decision for me: I yanked her off immediately.

We tried one more to no better effect, after which Tom and I decided that drugs were not for Charlotte. We had tired of adding guinea pig to her other difficult roles and decided to go au naturel.

We talked to her doctor, who seemed to feel we were being a bit hasty, although he didn't put up a big fuss. He was a rather well-known doctor, and I think he had treated hundreds of kids. He had told us that drugs didn't work for all kids, and, so, he didn't want to fight us when we said they weren't working for Charlotte.

Charlotte was happy when we took her off the drugs, too. At the beginning, we had told her that these pills would maybe make her concentrate better. She was compliant and agreed to try them, but she had never been able to concentrate well, so she wasn't all that enthusiastic about being able to do it better; she didn't seem to care much either way. But once the pills made her feel bad, she couldn't wait to get off of them. When we told her we'd be stopping the medication experiment, she didn't need any prodding.

I inadvertently got some much-needed perspective on the power of the meds when I once accidentally took one of Charlotte's Cylerts. I had been preoccupied when I was taking it out for her, and I just popped it absentmindedly as I might an aspirin. Well, within a half-hour, I felt like I was on Speed. My reaction was very different from Charlotte's but no more pleasant: for the next six hours, my mind raced, and I sat at my desk that day, feverishly typing at a hundred miles an hour! At one point, I felt that the drug was wearing off, and I breathed a sigh of relief—only to feel myself engulfed in another wave of speeding, followed by two more waves. In all, one tiny tablet had changed me dramatically for six hours. Wow. It seems so ironic that a drug like that, which makes you frenetic, can actually help some kids calm down and focus. Although I experienced a lot of discomfort that day, that's exactly what made the experience so eye-opening. I began to have a compassion for Charlotte that I had been lacking. But that was only the very beginning.

THE SCHOOL FOR MOMS

After four years at Gateway, Charlotte "aged out" of the school. She moved on to the Stephen Gaynor School on Manhattan's Upper West Side, one of the schools we'd rejected when we were first looking into them.

Gaynor was another wonderful place with kind, intelligent, attentive teachers who knew how to get through to kids like Charlotte. There were very few kids in each class—maybe six or seven. So, to a certain degree, it was possible for Charlotte's teachers to tailor their teaching to her specific issues. I have to give those teachers a lot of credit. Every case of LD is different, and every child has different needs. I don't know how they manage to help everyone so effectively, but they do.

The teachers at Gaynor really put me at ease, as well. I remember one particular occasion where one of them made a very strong impression on me as a compassionate soul. Tom and I were at the school for an early-morning parent conference. As we were finishing up, the kids started coming into the classroom. Charlotte stumbled in with her bulging backpack, laughing, not paying attention. As she moved into the room, she knocked over a desk. Then, as she turned around to see it crashing, her knapsack hit another desk, and it toppled over, too.

I knew this was going to happen from the minute I saw Charlotte enter the room. It was as if everything was happening in slow motion—I saw her moving in an unwieldy way, and I began to rise up from my chair to say, "Stop! Look out! You're going to knock things over!" I was embarrassed when the first desk fell. I got angry as the second desk started to fall. My blood pressure quickly rose. I couldn't have been more uptight about the havoc Charlotte was wreaking in public.

The teacher, Ms. Becker, on the other hand, handled the situation beautifully. She just laughed easily and said, "That's right, Charlotte. Knock 'em all down!" I was astounded and impressed by her level-headed, warm reaction. I thought, *That's what I should be doing—exuding love and acceptance, even when Charlotte is her most disorganized, chaotic LD self.* My whole body relaxed when I saw that Ms. Becker wasn't horrified or disapproving of that LD moment.

Ms. Becker was beautiful, intelligent, professional, and caring—a teacher from a Disney movie. I had admired her already, before the desks started tumbling. Unconsciously, I had been looking for role models who could show me how I should behave as a parent of a child with LD, how I should regard and treat Charlotte. Of course, I knew that as her mother, I had to fulfill her physical needs—to provide food and shelter and protect her as best I could. I knew it was also my job to get her all the help I could in the form of remediation and compensation from trained professionals. I could do those things. But despite my motherly love for her, I didn't know how to accept Charlotte completely. At the time, I only knew how to love her *in spite* of her LD. I needed to get to loving her *and* her LD. That morning, Ms. Becker modeled this for me. It was quite an epiphany.

FINDING COMPASSION

While I was grateful to Ms. Becker for demonstrating kindness and a healthy detachment from Charlotte's awkward ways that day, I was also forced to question myself. Why was it that this woman didn't get upset the way I did? What was my problem? Why was it that I found it so hard to express anger in most situations and with most people, but I had no problem snapping and losing my temper with Charlotte? She was an innocent. She didn't deserve this.

One of the biggest challenges for me as a parent of a child with learning differences has been managing my anger and finding compassion. So much about LD is utterly exasperating. It interferes with so much. Charlotte moves more slowly than anyone I know; she's disorganized and messy; she forgets things and has a difficult time communicating. For a normally functional person, it's like experiencing a system breakdown. It incites frustration and summons up anger.

Some of the things that Charlotte has found difficult over the years have seemed so easy and so basic that I've been stunned, not to mention impatient. For instance, dialing the phone was a huge challenge when Charlotte was in grade school. She just couldn't look at a telephone number on a page and dial it at the same time — or, more accurately, since we didn't have rotary phones, she couldn't punch the numbers on the keypad. She'd look at the page and then turn to the keypad. But by the time she punched in a digit or two, she would forget the other numbers on the page. She'd then turn back to the page, only to forget which numbers she'd already punched in. Of course, I'd be on the side, trying to breathe deeply and resist wrenching the phone out of her hands to dial it for her.

After a few failed attempts — and after I had some time to breathe and catch my temper — we'd try to break it down and make it easier for her: I would read her the numbers in groups of three. But that even was too much for her. I have to hand it to Charlotte for having the courage to speak up and say so, even though she must have felt embarrassed. She knew she needed all her concentration to find each individual number on the phone and to then summon her fine motor skills to press the right button, instead of the one next to it.

So, I would take a few more deep breaths, and we would break it down further, to one number at a time. I'd tell her "six" and she'd look around for "6." I'd see her eyes scanning all over. She'd find it. Then, I'd tell her "four," and she'd start all over again, looking for the number, as if she hadn't just scanned that same keypad a second ago looking for the "6." To my mind, this seemed impossible, and I'd find myself getting uptight; we were already on her third or fourth attempt at this one telephone number. Knowing what I do now about the way Charlotte's brain deals with numbers, I realize the key pad must have been completely overwhelming, with numbers and letters in one big puddle on the phone. But back then, I'd get anxious that if she didn't dial the next number quickly enough, that automated operator's voice would come on, saying, "Please hang up. A receiver appears to be off the hook . . . ," followed by a dial tone. And we'd have to start this infuriating process all over again.

BLOWING MY COVER

It was more than just the logistical difficulty and frustration of moments like those that got to me. There was something much deeper at work, causing me all of this distress.

What was going on inside me—what still sometimes goes on—was a frightening identification with my daughter and a feeling of being revealed as less than perfect. On the outside, I project a very together exterior: hard-working fashion designer of a popular label, happy wife and mother of two, with any unpleasant feelings neatly tucked in. But on the inside, I am messy. I am insecure, incomplete. I always feel I'm not the best I can be, not an "A." Underneath the glam exterior, I'm vulnerable, flawed, afraid, like everybody else. I have always been afraid of these very human emotions, and I've always done everything in my power to block them out.

Charlotte is the living embodiment of those aspects that I have a hard time acknowledging in myself, as well as of all the things I fear. When I see Charlotte stumble and fall—or bulldoze a few desks—I feel myself stumbling and falling with her. When she does something embarrassing, like moving in the opposite direction from all the other kids in a school dance number, I feel as if I'm there in the spotlight, looking and feeling foolish. Charlotte wears her vulnerability on the outside. I have worked my whole life to contain mine, and Charlotte interferes with that plan. She exposes me to myself, and that has been hard to deal with.

It's also been very good to deal with. I know now that this has been one of the most valuable aspects of my experience with Charlotte's LD. It was doing me no good to stay undercover and not deal with my true feelings, my true self. My journey has been twofold: I've watched Charlotte recognize, understand, and come to terms with her imperfections and fallibility, and I've recognized that human side of myself, as well as allowed the world—Tom, the rest of the family, the people I work with—to get to know these very real parts of me.

GIVE THE KID A BREAK

There was yet another layer to my emotional landscape: I felt sorry for Charlotte and angry that she had to bear the burden of her LD. She had to fail so publicly, so often. She had to deal with people who had no clue about learning differences and said stupid things to her. I remember a teenage boy at a pool who asked Annie very loudly, "Is your sister retarded?" because Charlotte had a hard time with whatever game it was they were playing. How painful it must have been for her—and Annie—to hear that.

Also, so much of Charlotte's free time was spent being tested and tutored and remediated and compensated. Nearly every day after school, she was schlepped—by me, Tom, or Monica—to doctors, tutors, and therapists of every stripe. There were the speech therapist and the occupational therapist. When she was nine, she began seeing a psychotherapist who specialized in helping kids with LD become more confident and learn to speak up for themselves—a good thing, but yet another of many appointments. There were endless psychological and neurological evaluations. There was barely time for her just to be a regular kid, and that broke my heart.

Not to mention that I often had to drag her around town. Sometimes I'd have to leave work, maybe at an important point in the design process, to make Charlotte's appointments. It would be hard to shift gears from work to LD and back to work. Actually, it was always easy to be in work mode; it was hard to shift out of it toward this new thing that I couldn't fully understand and that brought up floods of uncomfortable feelings for me.

Eventually, though, I started cutting down on Charlotte's intense schedule, reducing the number of appointments. And I started making room for fun.

Chapter 6

NATURE AND NURTURE

IMAGINE BEING DEFINED BY WHAT YOU'RE WORST AT—
being tone-deaf, always forgetting people's names, having aller-
gies. Doesn't seem very fair, does it?

But this is what happens to children with learning differences.
Their parents, and often the other people around them, see
them only as kids with LD.

Because LD affected every aspect of Charlotte's life—not just
her academics, but her social skills, athletic abilities, and more—
it was often difficult to see that there was a whole child there, one
not just with a mass of difficulties but with plenty of abilities as
well. Those abilities needed to be discovered and nurtured!

Over the years, I learned that it was not enough for me to be
a concerned, involved parent, always helping Charlotte get the
remediation and compensation she needed for her LD. I
needed to focus not only on her difficulties but also on her

strengths. My job as mom and chief executive of the Charlotte company was to search out and set free her gifts, her creativity, her abilities. I needed to put as much effort into identifying, nurturing, and encouraging her formidable strengths as I was putting into "fixing" and enhancing her. I needed to act as coach and cheering squad.

It wasn't easy, and I often lost my way. But one of my greatest sources of pride is that I eventually became those things for Charlotte.

A PORTRAIT OF THE
ARTIST AS A YOUNG GIRL

When Charlotte was really young, I was so freaked out by the prospect that something might be wrong that I became fixated on the things that seemed problematic—the odd speech, her awkward motion, her inability to count. Somehow, though, I managed not to miss something about her that was exceptional: her artistic abilities.

Her love of color and texture and her ability to convey ideas and feelings through images were apparent very early on. Charlotte was four or five, Annie two or three. I had begun a ritual with them that endured for many years: on Saturday mornings, before breakfast, the three of us would sit in the back room of the loft and make paper dolls at this big, gray design table I used for sketching my collections. I would break out my precious colored pencils, a Derwent set of 120 shades from my days studying fashion design at St. Martin's in London. Tom might be sleeping late or jogging (we took turns getting up early), and after a couple of hours, he'd go to the kitchen and make pancakes for his hungry artist girls.

I loved our time in this back room. The girls were in good moods, refreshed by sleep. We always had lots of art supplies—every color of pencil imaginable, stacks of recycled paper, scissors, tape—all right there. It was a great way for us to spend time together, being creative, after I had been working so hard all week and not terribly available to them. I'd sit in the middle and would place a girl on each side. Each had her own drawer to keep her supplies in. I'd turn on my beloved National Public Radio, and we'd draw for hours in relative silence.

On one side of me, little Annie often drew girls with big round faces, no necks, and straight hair down to their feet. She loved to sharpen her pencils down to a nub, laughing and laughing as they got to be her ideal one-inch length. Later, she got a plastic stencil with letters and would trace the letters for hours. She wrote her name in upper case, with the "e" looking like a comb with many teeth.

On my other side, Charlotte was developing a whole population of paper dolls. She would often draw the whole thing herself—face, body, and wild clothes (budding designers start early!). Together we'd make up complex stories and characters. I still have boxes full of her wild creations, each doll with a name and a complete story, including the "stars" of our paper doll soap opera, Paul and Tanya. They're tattered and funny looking but evoke strong, pleasurable memories, each one.

PURE JOY

Charlotte has always been a different person when she's making art—fully focused and engaged, yet with her body completely relaxed, as if in a wonderful "zone." From the beginning, everything related to art came easily to and pleased her. Her artistic self has always been exuberant and happy, and I've loved observing her in this state.

Luckily, I, too, enjoy art projects. Whenever there was time, in addition to our Saturday morning paper doll sessions, we'd enjoy many creative endeavors. What started with crayons progressed to finger paint—how I loved that slick paper and gooey paint. At that time, our furniture was still neohippie, so I was relaxed about making a mess. (Our loft only got fancier three years ago, when the girls were fifteen and thirteen. By then, Annie had stopped doing craft projects, and Charlotte had gotten more careful. I still try to contain any real mess: I insist on the use of lots of newspaper under the paint projects but still allow them to go on just about everywhere.) Finger painting was also a perfect activity for an artistically inclined LD kid, her little sister, and her stressed-out mother—you dip and smear; the paint is cool and viscous; it slips and goes on easily. The tactile sensations guide the creative process. Hand-eye coordination is the farthest thing from a factor—it is more like finger-dancing. More importantly, since there was no way to "succeed," there was no way "fail."

We advanced from finger paints to markers to tempera paint. Eventually, we did everything—watercolor painting, ink drawing, gouache, ceramics, batik, linoleum block printing, and air brushing. A friend and neighbor, also the mom of two girls Charlotte and Annie's ages, came over one weekend morning when we were happily making art and a mess at our dining room table and said, "I can't believe it. Every time I come by, every single time, you all are doing art projects! Don't you ever want to do something else?" Well, actually, we didn't. We all loved doing art. And it turned out to be a great thing for Charlotte.

Art became something Charlotte, Annie, and I could do together, that we all enjoyed, that the three of us could do happily. There was no competition, no right or wrong. The girls had completely different styles—each has real talent.

Charlotte's free-form approach to things translated beautifully into art projects. Watching her work was fascinating: she didn't plan. She didn't spend time thinking things through. The moment she sat down, she would dive into a creation *immediately*. Pick up the pencil and start drawing. No hesitations. No false starts. Very few erasures. She just let her instincts guide her, without getting hung up on neatness or precision. There were no voices in her head or critics on her shoulder saying, "Do it this way." Nothing hampered her total immersion. The abandon and confidence with which she threw herself into whatever medium we chose was wonderful to behold. Her wild color sense and unfettered imagination yielded dramatic, evocative pieces.

ART THERAPY

As time went on and Charlotte grew, our connection with art, and with each other through art, grew even stronger. It was even what we did together in ski lodges while Tom and Annie skied.

But it wasn't just a way for us to bond. After a while, I realized there was a therapeutic benefit, too: after the school year's long challenges and trials, weekends and summers filled with art were relaxing and affirming for Charlotte. To delve into something she loved and to do well at it, to realize that there was an area in which her skills were not wanting, but in which she was quite gifted, was a wonderful thing for her. Here was the playing field on which she could shine.

When she was a little older, we realized it would be a good idea to help Charlotte further develop her artistic gifts, so when she was sixteen, we sent her to an arts summer sleep-away camp that may as well have been created just for her. In rural Connecticut, Buck's Rock Camp was founded by people who didn't believe in a rigid, structured camping experience.

The whole camp was all about art, with minimal sports and absolutely no required activities. Each day, twenty-eight different art studios were open, staffed by working artists. Campers could choose what they wanted to do each day, change whenever they wanted, go to all different studios or to none.

The minute we drove up, Charlotte seemed right at home. The kids were not LD but were an open, tolerant, nonjudgmental group. I felt I was back in the late 1960s: I saw lots of bohemian attire, with tie-dye everywhere, long skirts, long hair, unkempt clothes, multiple piercings, green hair—zero preppy penetration. These weren't the cookie-cutter New York City private school kids Charlotte never felt comfortable around. This was her kind of place. It's no surprise to me that she thrived socially, as well as artistically, for two summers there. That experience went a long way toward building Charlotte's confidence as an artist and helping her expand her talents.

There was only one incident at Buck's Rock that was difficult for Charlotte. At one point, a jewelry instructor asked her group to measure something on a ruler, an impossible task for Charlotte related to her difficulty with numbers. She just couldn't do it. She tried to explain it to the counselor, who was annoyed and just wasn't getting it. Charlotte wound up in tears, back in her bunk. It's painful to recall that story. Charlotte hadn't had to let anyone at that camp know she had learning differences, up to that point. She had been feeling "normal" and enjoying doing well at her art.

This incident at Buck's Rock took some of the wind out of Charlotte's sails. She didn't tell me about it over the phone—our phone calls were not very newsy; they were noncommittal at best, mopey at worst. But after I picked her up at the end of camp, she told me all about it. Her eyes welled up as she remembered her mortification. She had said nothing to the jewelry instructor but had left abruptly, gone back to her bunk, and sobbed by herself. I asked if she had told anyone, and she said she later told her cabin counselor—the one with five piercings on her face and hair that looked like it had been cut with a hacksaw but who was kind and empathetic and knew when another human being was hurting.

Charlotte was embarrassed that the teacher hadn't understood her LD, mortified that she had talked to her sharply like that. The experience had taken her by surprise, and she never went back to the studio. It somewhat soured her other positive camp experiences, of which there were many. It reminded her that even in an idyllic camp atmosphere, her LD would haunt her, track her down, and make her feel diminished.

EXPERIENCING TECHNICAL DIFFICULTIES

Yes, even art, an area in which Charlotte shines, is affected by her LD. Everything is affected by it.

When we first started making those paper dolls when she was young, the whole thing came naturally to her with the exception

of one detail: I had to do most of the cutting because she had serious trouble with managing scissors. Fine motor coordination
was a weak point: her hands would shake, and she had a hard
time coordinating right and left.

For years, when cutting, Charlotte would hold the scissors still
and move the paper through them, instead of the opposite, more
accepted way. Being a lefty didn't make it any easier. As a very
young child, she didn't mind that the cutting was ragged and out
of the lines—her imagination was so strong that the "rightness"
of the creation in her mind was all that mattered. But after she
had been attending school for a while, and she had noticed from
her younger sister Annie's meticulous style of drawing and cutting that there were other ways to create paper dolls, she started
to wonder if hers were not as perfect as they seemed in her mind.
I remember when she started questioning, ever so slightly holding back her exuberance, when that shadow of "Oh, are these in-
ferior?" first passed across her face. She started handing the dolls
to me to cut out for her.

It dawned on me that I should speak to Charlotte's first-grade
teacher at Gateway about this. When I did, she pointed out that
cutting provided an important opportunity for someone like
Charlotte to strengthen her fine motor skills—that I should not
brush it off as an unimportant life skill. Prior to that, I had been
thinking, *How many CEO's or real estate salespeople or astro-
nauts cut things out—so what if Charlotte is not good at it?* The
teacher stressed that the hours Charlotte spent struggling with
cutting would serve her well as she gradually gained more control over her shaky fingers. And rather than just seeing this as
something that should be "fixed" at school, she showed me that
it was something I could help Charlotte with. She coached me

not to do the cutting for her. I learned that I would be serving Charlotte best if I would sit by, encourage her, help steady her hands, guide her to move the scissors instead of the paper.

Oh, how difficult it was not to just do it for her! It was so hard to watch her struggle. It was *painful*. That, and my patience would often wear thin.

But this is what I had to do. *I* was learning, too—learning how to coach Charlotte and how to let even commonplace activities become a chance for her to learn to do things for herself.

NO SUCH THING AS QUALITY TIME

I was also beginning to learn how important it was for me to be involved in Charlotte's education. I suddenly saw that I needed to make time to get to understand Charlotte better at home and also to interact with her teachers more.

But time was not something I had a lot of. When Charlotte and Annie were young, so was the Dana Buchman label. I was an ambitious young designer, building recognition for my brand.

I worked like a maniac all week long. When there wasn't enough time in the day, I'd get up and work some more, between 2 and 4 a.m. I spent countless hours putting together the new collection every season, not to mention traveling to Asia, Europe, and around the United States several times a year. Nothing was too much to attempt if it seemed like the right thing for my label. No matter how big the task seemed, I'd straighten my already erect posture, roll up my sleeves, and just make it happen.

And looking back now, I wish I had reprioritized my time.

This is what gets me: I sometimes even worked while I was spending time with Charlotte and Annie! Those wonderful

Saturday mornings we spent drawing together and making paper dolls—how many of those mornings did I turn my attention away from the girls while they were sitting with me to go over sketches and paperwork and answer Telex messages (the Telex was a clunky machine that predated the fax). I cringe when I think about how much I let my perfectionism and workaholism interfere with that special time.

I also wasn't as available as I should have been for the little mundane things that add up to a lot. I remember once walking the girls to the Montessori nursery school in our neighborhood on my way to work. I tried to walk them to the school's door at least once a week—how big of me. One day, either Charlotte or Annie looked up at me and said, "Mom, no one knows you." I thought to myself, what do you mean? A lot of people know me. They wear my clothes; they come to my fashion shows. She continued, "I mean at school. None of the kids or teachers know what you look like. The other mothers stop in and visit, but no one knows who you are." I can still feel the pangs of guilt and regret. Once again, I was paying dearly for trying to "have it all."

I really wasn't giving the girls the attention they needed. Charlotte, in particular, needed me to be more involved. It is astounding how time-consuming LD is. I wish I had had a warning, someone telling me, "Hey, Dana, buckle your seatbelt. This is going to be quite a long ride." Even beyond all the appointments with doctors and tutors and therapists, I needed to leave time for interacting with Charlotte, one on one, for getting to know her more deeply. We needed to play together, snuggle, and, above all, have conversations. I had to hear what she had to say about what it was like to struggle the way she did. I also had to observe the way her mind operated, the way she learned.

And to do this, I needed to devote time, and not just any "time," but time with my full attention. The Catch 22 of working mothers—*Am I short-changing my child?*—haunts LD moms tenfold.

GETTING TO KNOW MY OWN CHILD

Each child is different, and so is every case of LD. Because Charlotte was unique, no one would be able to teach me about her mind the way she could.

I had to spend time just noticing how she did things, how she processed information, how she expressed herself. For example, when Charlotte was in elementary school, I noticed that she was more "on" on some days than on others. Maybe for a couple of weeks, her scissor-cutting or writing or reading would seem more fluent, less choppy and hesitant. Then, all of a sudden, I would notice a decline. For one week or several, she would seem more handicapped, unable to control her movements or to direct them as she meant to. A few weeks later, she'd be "on" again. I came to realize that this rhythm was just a part of Charlotte.

I also noticed that Charlotte had a tendency to get exhausted over the course of her school day, to the point that she'd practically collapse before getting on the school bus home. This may not seem like it had anything to do with LD, but I'm pretty sure it did. Because she's challenged in ways that other kids aren't, because she has to work so much harder to learn in school, because she has physical-coordination issues and has to think and work through nearly all her moves, Charlotte got wiped out more easily than other kids. Add to that her speedy, birdlike metabolism, and it's no wonder she'd arrive home from school like a wet rag.

I came up with a solution: I gave the teachers at Charlotte's school snacks and juice boxes to hand to Charlotte toward the end of the school day to revive her. I also learned to keep the house stocked with healthy snacks to bring her back to life once she got home. This may seem very simple and obvious, like Parenting 101, but it was very specific to Charlotte, and my attention to her end-of-day energy deficit made it easier for her to do her homework and otherwise function once she got home.

TEACHING THE TEACHERS

I remember one Saturday when Charlotte was about nine or ten. I had been embroidering with her, using lovely lightweight muslin, comfortably dull embroidery needles, beautiful jewel-toned thread, and the wooden embroidery hoops I had used with my grandmother as a little girl. Charlotte was enjoying the project, but, not surprisingly, she was having a difficult time managing her hands and all the elements. I ended up holding the hoops for her and pointing where to jab in the needle. She mentioned that she was doing sewing at school as part of occupational therapy (OT). This was a surprise to me. I hadn't thought of needlework as therapeutic, only as pleasurable. I had what seemed like a brilliant and unique idea: I'd talk to the OT teacher to see if she had any thoughts about or tips for guiding Charlotte in the pursuit of one of my favorite things.

When I walked in at the time of my appointment, the very friendly, warm OT teacher greeted me with, "It's about time."

"What do you mean?" I asked.

"I was wondering when you would make an appointment to see me. Most of the parents are calling or in here all the time."

I was a little stunned and even taken aback, but I swallowed my pride, and we talked for almost an hour about Charlotte's strengths and weaknesses and how Charlotte's and my play could provide good therapy for her fine-motor-skill development. As I left, she reminded me gently, "Remember, it's good to be in our faces. Be a squeaky wheel—stay connected."

She was not advising me to become a frantic, meddling, complaining, second-guessing parent. (Over the years, I have witnessed pushy parents like that. All they do is alienate the hardworking teachers and therapists, which ultimately affects their child's education.) The OT teacher was letting me know that parents of LD kids need to stay engaged at the school more so than parents of kids in mainstream schools. The teachers and administrators need to know the parent is involved and interested. Just dropping the kids off at the door and paying the bills is not enough.

I'm embarrassed to say, this was a revelation for me. I thought a good parent turned her kid's education over to the professionals and let them run with it. I was beginning to see that partnering with Charlotte's teachers was not only helpful but essential.

I was so energized by this epiphany that I made an appointment with the staff psychologist at the Gaynor School, where Charlotte went at the time. The school psychologist there oversees not only the children's emotional status but their learning status as well. When I walked in the door, she also greeted me warmly. Then she said, "We were wondering when you were going to come in." Not just "I was wondering" but "we," as if my absence had been a whole topic of conversation there! I felt humiliated and ashamed. How could I not know that I needed to be more involved? Where was my head? In my office on Seventh Avenue, probably.

As I began to talk more with Charlotte's teachers and the administrators at her school, a fuller picture of my daughter began to emerge. The teachers and I got to see that there were parts of Charlotte, ways she behaved, that she reserved for home, and others she reserved for school.

For example, Charlotte has always been a compliant child—from the beginning she was an ideal student in that she was quiet, obeyed the rules, did her homework, and was interested in learning. Sometimes this model behavior tricked the teachers into thinking that everything they were teaching was getting through. They had no idea about the many times Charlotte would burst into tears of frustration at home, complaining, "I don't understand this. I didn't understand a thing that went on today, and it's so frustrating." I have had several meetings with well-intentioned teachers who were shocked to learn that Charlotte's attentive demeanor hid confusion and anguish.

Sometimes, though, no matter how involved we got with the teachers, certain things weren't easily resolved—like Charlotte's inability to read an analog clock. Tom and I talked to Charlotte's teachers for four years, starting in fourth grade, about this. We pushed, nudged, insisted that this was an important life skill. As a seventh grader, Charlotte would bring home math homework dealing with decimals but still could not read the hands of a clock. No number of meetings with teachers was going to solve this problem. To this day, I'm not sure whether Charlotte can tell the time if it's not displayed digitally. She stares at clocks, tilts her head, and I don't really know what she thinks.

THE D WORD

This may seem hard to believe, but with all the attention we as a family paid to Charlotte's learning differences, we almost never talked about them as a family. That was a big mistake. It gave Annie and Charlotte the feeling that the topic was off limits, taboo. And I think it reinforced for Charlotte the feeling that LD was something really bad, something embarrassing or shameful.

Of course, Tom and I would discuss LD strategy among ourselves—what doctors to see when—but even we didn't delve deeply into the emotional aspects of it. And we never discussed any of it in front of the girls. This was partly avoidance of a topic Tom and I were uncomfortable with. But it was also a conscious decision. Until she was nine years old, we hadn't yet told Charlotte she had LD because her school advised against telling her when she was so young. There is a camp of thought within the LD field that suggests it is a mistake to label a child. I've even read that labeling isn't advisable for so-called normal kids because it can be limiting. You don't want to say, "You're a good runner"; you want to say, "You ran fast."

Ironically, we told Annie about Charlotte's LD first. Annie was reaching a point where she could tell something was amiss. She was puzzled and confused and just needed to know.

Tom was the one who explained it to Annie, privately. Annie was five or six, and Tom took her for a walk, carrying her lovingly on his shoulders.

"Annie, have you ever noticed that Charlotte has trouble with certain things?" he asked.

Annie nodded. Although she was barely school age and two years younger than her big sister, Annie was very sharp and had discerned Charlotte's difficulty handling scissors, lacing things up, writing clearly, moving her piece correctly along the Candy Land board. Annie knew that she was already able to read and write better than Charlotte. She was aware of Charlotte's frustration and her disappointment. But this was the first time it had been acknowledged to Annie in a conversation.

"Charlotte has what are called 'learning disabilities,'" Tom explained to Annie. "It's harder for her to learn to do some things than it is for you." (Yes, back then we were still saying "disabilities" instead of "differences." We didn't know better.)

I wasn't on that walk, but, boy, do I wish I could have been a fly on Tom's shoulder. All I know is that when they returned from their walk, I witnessed a huge sense of relief in them both, which helped me, too. Finally, talking about LD, even just that beginning of a conversation, rather than pretending there wasn't a huge elephant in the room, released a lot of tension.

When we first told Charlotte about her LD, we did it in private, too, still keeping it hush-hush.

Looking back, I wish we had handled it differently. We should have told Charlotte and Annie at the same time—given it a name, a verbal acknowledgement of something all four of us knew was there.

Once Charlotte knew, I remember her asking us where she got this LD from, a question she'd come to ask again and again. "Who else in the family has it?" she'd beg later on. It wasn't that she wanted someone to blame it on; she wanted to know that she had company in the family, that she wasn't the only one who struggled with this difference. She didn't want to imagine the family tree with absolutely no LD anywhere except on her branch.

Eventually we started using the term *LD*, or *learning disability*, around the house — rather awkwardly. I tried to use the words deliberately, and they stuck in my throat. I'd get tight around my neck. And even after I said them, the words felt like they were just sitting there, in the room. They seemed to hurt. We even brought "it" up at the dinner table once or twice. Yes, those family conversations were awkward and painful for all four of us.

Charlotte would say, "Annie's good at reading and writing and board games and sports. What am I good at?"

And we'd say, "You're good at art."

And she'd say, glancing at Annie, "Well, what else?"

We'd answer, "Well, you're able to talk to adults in a way most kids can't. And you're sensitive to people. And you try hard."

The list of skills Charlotte was good at, or, more importantly, better at than Annie, never seemed adequate, at least not in terms of abilities and traits that can be measured by schools and that our society considers to be most valuable. Charlotte felt sad, Annie felt guilty, and all four of us felt depressed and anxious to leave the discussion and never come back to it. A feeling of shame became attached to LD.

Why couldn't we come up with an adequate list of skills? I knew I loved Charlotte fiercely. That was never the question. But when you're listing for your child skills and assets that the world admires at that age, for some reason, being lovable and loving seem to come up short, as did being incredibly perceptive, empathetic, and hardworking. That's nuts, of course. Why *doesn't* our society appreciate genuineness, warmth, and emotional intelligence in children? Is it because these aren't quantifiable attributes, ones we can measure? Whatever the reason, these traits aren't valued, especially during the school years, and I think that's a shame. These were some of Charlotte's strongest suits.

But how do you explain that to a little kid who wants to know why her little sister is achieving in ways that she can't? You can see why LD would be a difficult family topic.

We're still trying to learn how to talk about LD and all the emotional stuff attached to it. But part of what we're doing is just learning to talk openly as a family about things that are uncomfortable. Little by little, we are making strides. But I wish we could get there faster and that all along we had talked more — constantly, honestly.

Chapter 7

IT'S A FAMILY AFFAIR

IN WAYS I COULDN'T HAVE IMAGINED WHEN WE FIRST learned of Charlotte's differences, LD affects the whole family. No one and nothing could have prepared me for the issues that we as a family would come to face.

Of course, I realized immediately that having LD would affect Charlotte. And I could feel how it was affecting Tom and me—roiling our emotions and challenging our assumptions on so many fronts. But I had no idea how much it would affect Annie, the non-LD sibling, and how much impact it would have on the family dynamics overall.

Every family has its issues and challenges. Even without LD in the mix, of course, we would naturally have had emotional obstacles to tackle. That's just family life—four different people with four different personalities and sets of needs under one roof, growing through all sorts of changes over time. And "issues" aren't altogether a bad thing. It's often issues that bring a family closer together. That is the case with ours.

But, along the way to that closeness, there were some very trying times, and the presence of LD made them more trying.

THE HAPPY COUPLE

For better or for worse, as the marriage vows say, LD has had an impact on my relationship with Tom.

It brought up all sorts of emotions neither of us were equipped to deal with. Our inability to face our feelings made us each protect ourselves in our own ways—me, by throwing myself headlong into my work and always acting perky, even when I was feeling anxious and upset on the inside; Tom, by filling up all his free time with so many extracurricular athletic adventures that there was minimal opportunity to reflect on uncomfortable feelings.

Of course, we didn't do this consciously. Neither of us had any idea that we had our defenses up or what those defenses looked like. But they began to grow like a wall of unspoken words between us.

For years, when Tom and I would talk about Charlotte's LD, we would concentrate on what to do or how she was doing in school or in speech therapy. We would often talk about it as we lay in bed at night. We'd read for a bit, then put our books down and discuss whatever was going on at the time—in a very matter-of-fact manner. I'd say something like, "Charlotte had a good meeting with Leda Molly today." And Tom would say, "She did? That's great." Then, I would say, "You know, maybe she should see her twice a week when school starts," and he'd respond, "Yeah, that may be a good idea."

There we were, figuratively sipping tea with extended pinkies and having a polite conversation, while, on the inside, we were each experiencing an Armageddon of emotions.

Sometimes, we'd discuss it as we made coffee in the morning. Neither of us enjoyed the topic. It was difficult, confusing, disturbing. We never knew what exactly we should be doing for Charlotte as her LD needs kept changing as she grew. We'd force ourselves to discuss our choices, our options. As soon as we felt we'd come to a plan of action, we'd move on to a less difficult topic.

Over time, what we left unsaid silently drew us apart. I don't think Tom and I had any idea that we were slowly drifting. It was something that began when Charlotte was born (just having kids naturally puts strain on a marriage) but picked up pace when LD appeared in our life. On the surface, we seemed like a perfect couple. We were both successful in our careers. We had two beautiful children. We valued the same things—honesty, loyalty, family. And we "got along " beautifully.

We were also very aligned in our approach toward helping Charlotte, something I've heard is quite uncommon. I've read that fathers often go into denial about their kids having LD and think it isn't something real. Not so with Tom.

Most notably, though, we never fought. I know now that this isn't the admirable, great thing that I thought it was at the time. It would have been an okay thing—even a good thing—to argue and get mad at each other from time to time. Hard as it may be to believe, through therapy—individual and couples—I have only in the past few years learned that disagreeing and revealing uncomfortable feelings is infinitely healthier than the well-behaved restraining of emotions in which Tom and I were both so heavily invested. But more about that later!

In recent years, we've begun opening up more to each other about our feelings about everything, including LD. There's a certain level of closeness you can't reach with your partner unless you're both willing to reveal your vulnerabilities to one another. We're really just learning to do this; there's still a certain degree to which we can't always connect about LD. It sometimes sits there, between us. Even at this late date, it remains a difficult topic for us to touch at a very intimate level. In time, though, I believe it will get easier.

It's still difficult talking about LD with the girls, too. It's silly because talking about it is probably the one thing that would make LD less daunting for us all. In our family, and I'm sure in many others as well, LD is often the big pink elephant sprawled out across the living room floor that everyone notices and tiptoes around but neglects to mention. We've made strides in this area—we can talk about it *a little bit,* from time to time, usually if Charlotte has brought it up in some way.

DIVIDED ATTENTION

That big pink elephant often plops itself down right between Charlotte and Annie. There, I suppose, it gets noticed the most, by the girls. They are equally uncomfortable with its presence, and both are uncomfortable acknowledging outwardly that it's there.

But it's there, alright. It always has been, from the time Annie appeared on the scene, when Charlotte was two.

A couple of years later, when we started making those paper dolls together on Saturday mornings in the back of the loft, before Charlotte's LD had even been completely diagnosed, there it was, creating an imbalance in the room. Because Charlotte had difficulty holding and maneuvering the scissors, I wound up putting just about all of my energy and focus into helping her. And practically ignored Annie.

I feel so sad when I recall that part of it—to the point where it is almost too painful for me to write about. I am afraid of betraying Annie by writing for the world the sadness we have not really spoken of much at home. It is so painfully vivid to me—my back to little three-year-old Annie, who somehow understood that her older sister needed more help, although she quietly yearned for my attention.

Annie has always been independent. She could do things herself. She could cut accurately at an early age, could and would climb down from the high chair and go and get something she needed. But that didn't mean she didn't need some of her mother's attention, especially at such a young age.

Throughout their childhood years, because Charlotte needed me more in very basic ways, I never gave Annie enough time or attention, and it haunts me. Only now, in her mid teens, is Annie able to begin articulating how very difficult that was for her and to tap into her feelings of sadness and anger about it.

Of course, sibling rivalry is as old as time. No sibling has ever felt she got full attention from her parents, no matter how much the parents struggled to make sure they divided their energy and attention evenly among their kids.

But where one of the children has differences and absolutely needs more help, and another child doesn't have those differences and achieves more, making sure everyone feels fulfilled and acknowledged is a constant challenge. Even now, with the girls in their late teens, we still encounter this challenge all the time in our household. I try to be aware of it, but it's a tricky, pernicious little beast that sneaks up when you're not looking.

EVERYONE LOSES

Not only did Annie have to live without the kind of doting that Charlotte received, but she also learned to downplay her successes and triumphs at school and on playing fields. (Granted, she also didn't have to live with the sense that her parents were disappointed with her, the way that Charlotte did.) In certain ways, Annie couldn't be more opposite from Charlotte. She's an academic overachiever in one of the most competitive high schools in the city. She's also an accomplished athlete, who is always up for a challenge in just about any sport.

To be very honest, Tom and I made very little fuss over Annie's straight A's and athletic trophies because we had it in our minds that we shouldn't make grades and awards seem so important to our kids. Now, where did we get that idea? I believe it came, at least in part, from having a child with LD, who couldn't bring home the kind of bacon other kids could.

But I think Tom and I took that notion too far and made Annie feel unappreciated, especially since we made a big deal over most of Charlotte's achievements. When Charlotte brought home a good report card, we laid it on thick. Charlotte struggles with a low confidence level, a byproduct of LD, so we've always felt we needed to give her tremendous support, which we never quite matched for Annie.

What's even more damaging than the fact that we didn't vo-
cally admire Annie's triumphs is that somewhere, subliminally,
we gave her the sense that we actually valued them *too much.* I
wonder whether, underneath, she feels responsible for fulfilling
our parental dreams, and that's why she sometimes feels driven
to go beyond what her own preferences might be.

We gave Annie the impression that her role is strictly to succeed; she's not allowed to have weaknesses or vulnerabilities.
That's Charlotte's department, even though we all know everyone has these. I regret that Annie's insecurities weren't addressed
and nursed the way Charlotte's were.

Don't get me wrong: I didn't ignore Annie totally. Of course,
I delighted in her triumphs, and I spent a lot of time listening to
her own trials and frustrations. But things were lopsided. It was
something we fell into inadvertently. I wasn't as observant as I
should have been. Between running my business, raising two
kids who were two years apart, and managing Charlotte's LD,
many days I felt like a triage medic taking care of what needed
immediate attention.

So, even with the best of intentions, we fell into a pattern in
which, oddly enough, both girls came up short. In getting so
much attention for her pain and anguish, Charlotte did not receive enough gentle prodding, encouraging, or outright pushing
to do things herself. I often erred on the side of supporting to the
point of enabling her insecurities. As with all children, it's important for LD kids to feel supported, but it's equally important
that they feel their parents have confidence that they can do
things for themselves.

And in my effort not to make Charlotte feel badly for not
being able to do certain things, I know I sold Annie short. It is

only in the writing of this book that I have learned about some of the very private ways Annie has dealt with her feelings about this—like secretly photocopying Charlotte's work and hers so that, someday, someone would appreciate the discrepancy and acknowledge her for her ability and effort.

The truth is, I was always very proud of Annie, but I was anxious to hide from Charlotte, from Annie, and from myself my joy in Annie's A's and athletic skills. I had learned from Charlotte's situation that it's not a good idea to place too much emphasis on achievement, that there's much more to a person than what they can do. But, I realize now, that doesn't mean that one can't delight in a child's gifts and well-earned markers of success.

THE BREAKING POINT

Tom and I were talking recently, and he brought up how hard it must be for each of the girls—how difficult it must be for Charlotte to have her younger sister reach many milestones before she does, and how awkward it must be for Annie, as the younger sister, to lead. Annie often feels like the older sister, and Charlotte, like the younger. It's funny—I remember now that when they used to play house, Charlotte always got to be the mother or the big sister. They seemed to be agreeing to let Charlotte play the role she was supposed to, as determined by birth order.

Life isn't fair, especially when you put LD into the mix. It isn't fair to have LD when your sibling doesn't, and that leads to anger and jealousy, on top of the frustration and anguish that come with LD in the first place. It's also not fair to be a sibling of an LD child. You have to watch your parents devote an inordinate amount of time and attention to the "different" child, and that incites anger and jealousy, not to mention guilt for being the "normal" one.

A few years ago, Annie got very angry that Charlotte consistently came home from school with much less homework than she. Just getting through the school day is a huge challenge for Charlotte. There's so much for her to negotiate: finding her way to and from her special school, managing conversations with different people, absorbing the lessons of the day. By the time she gets home, she's listless and she needs a nap. Annie, on the other hand, goes to one of the most competitive private schools in New York City; she's involved in after-school sports and other extracurricular activities. And when she gets home, she faces hours upon hours of challenging homework in all of her subjects.

One day, Annie said to Charlotte, "It's not fair! How come you don't have to do as much work as I do? I come home and do homework for hours and hours, and you only have a very little bit to do."

Charlotte was completely taken aback. She paused a minute and then said, "Oh, really? You think I have it easy? You want to be me?"

Who won that battle? Neither of them.

Lately, the deep-seated resentments on both their parts are coming to the surface more often. This is actually good news! Better to air things, we are all learning.

For example, one evening the year before Charlotte went off to college, we were all gathered at home for dinner. Annie came to the table from doing her calculus homework and was explaining something she found interesting about the delta function. I vaguely followed the gist of what she was saying, calling up remnants of what I had learned in calculus through the fog of thirty-five years, but I was not able to engage in the details of it. I enjoyed that she was excited about it, but when everyone came to the dinner table, the talk turned to other things.

More specifically, our talk turned to Charlotte's acceptance to Curry College, one of the few colleges that has a really comprehensive LD program. Tom and I were congratulating her and sharing her enjoyment at having been accepted, especially because Charlotte had been agonizing over whether she'd get into any schools with her very low SAT scores. And she had been feeling awkward about telling people the unfamiliar names of the colleges that had LD programs, which she was waiting to hear from. Annie, meanwhile, was already looking at "name" schools like Brown, Harvard, and Dartmouth, which depressed Charlotte.

As dinner ended that evening, and Annie left the table to start her homework, I could sense something was wrong, so I followed her into her room. I don't remember how she started, but it became clear very quickly that she was angry. She said, "You all get so excited at every little thing that Charlotte does, like writing her paper. But then when I get an A– in Calculus, which I think is pretty good, you say, 'Oh, that's nice.' And you say things like 'Well, I took Calculus and forgot it the day the class ended, and it's not something I've ever used anyway.' So it makes it seems like this thing I'm interested in has no value. I don't get the credit for the things I do well, and yet Charlotte gets credit for things she does well. In fact, she gets credit for just even trying to do things. I get a high score on the PSAT and you say, 'That's nice.'"

My spine went cold. I knew exactly what she was talking about. Annie was right. I have often minimized the importance of her achievements. My twisted reasoning went this way: if Annie worked hard and made A's in very difficult subjects, and I got overly excited, I would belie the story I was telling Charlotte and myself that grades and academic achievement don't matter.

I have always told the girls that grades don't matter, that if they do their homework and do their best, then that's enough. I always asked if they knew what grades I made in high school biology. Or what I got on my SAT's. Of course not, they'd say. And neither did anyone else in the world, certainly not the women who buy my clothes. What do they care about how well I did in calculus? Although I did well in school, grades ultimately never affected my career or my life with Tom or with my friends.

But I carried way too far my commitment to telling the girls that their achievement in school did not matter to me, that trying to do the work and enjoying the learning were what was important. In putting across that message to Annie, I failed to delight in her academic and athletic gifts in the way I delighted in Charlotte's unconventional, nonacademic gifts. I didn't make it clear that I loved that she skis like the wind, gracefully and confidently. That she learns easily and enjoys her prowess. And that she has always been kind and patient with her sister. But, for every frustration of Annie's, Charlotte had two. Some of the most basic things were huge challenges for her—things like keeping up with the conversation at dinner.

For a long time, we didn't realize Charlotte was having a hard time keeping up with us in conversation and that we needed to create openings for her. At the dinner table, Tom and Annie and I would just start rattling off what our days were like, talking quickly, using big words, and Charlotte would sit there, dumbfounded, not knowing how to organize her thoughts and get a word in edgewise. We finally realized that we needed to make the space for her to speak. But then we ran into another problem: Charlotte would take up the whole dinner hour telling a story. And now there was no way for anyone else to talk. How could we kindly and gently rein her in, after working so hard to make it easier for her to speak up, so that the rest of us got a chance to contribute to the dinner conversation? It was tricky.

Charlotte also has to live with constantly measuring herself against her little sister. I remember the night that Annie came back from taking the written test for her driver's permit. Charlotte had taken it a few months before and just passed. At dinner that night, Charlotte asked Annie, "So, how many questions did you get wrong?" It was a loaded question, and we were all silent for a moment before Annie quietly answered. Of course, Annie got a perfect score on the exam. Of course, Charlotte, who had barely passed the test herself, suspected that. Charlotte was venting her anger by provoking Annie's guilt.

MANAGING

So, how do you handle all this emotional mess? For one thing, I got help. I'm a fan of professional help: call in a designer when you need help getting dressed, and call in a shrink when you need help figuring out a psychological issue!

At one point, when Annie was six, it became impossible to dismiss the fact that she and I weren't getting along. I took her to see Charlotte's neuropsychologist, even though Annie wasn't the one with neurological issues.

It was like we were in couples counseling, my daughter and I. We were angry at each other, and we didn't know why. The neuropsychologist, Michele, had Annie draw a picture. Annie drew a tree whose leaves had all turned brown and fallen to the ground. (It makes me teary even to write that.) To a psychological professional, that is a loud and clear message of sadness in a little person. From that, I learned that Charlotte's needs were overshadowing Annie's, especially for attention and acknowledgment. This was the beginning of my awareness of the imbalance in our family loft.

Probably the best remedy for that imbalance has been making time for Charlotte and Annie separately. I started to realize that it was often easier, and a richer experience for me, to be with one child at a time. I would take each of them out individually on a weekend afternoon. I would take extra time putting them each to bed at night, something that was difficult because I got so little sleep myself. I was often up from 2 to 4 a.m. sketching because it was the only time when it was peaceful enough for me to relax and free-associate creatively. I also often had to get up at crazy hours to speak with our offices in Asia.

Indeed, my work was everpresent, but in one respect, I managed to combine it with the needs of each of my daughters: I'd let each of the girls take turns traveling with me to trunk shows around the country. In that environment, I could pamper each of them, one at a time. The trip would usually include a limousine ride, room service, a bubble bath, and then the excitement of joining me for my appearance at a store. For Charlotte, this was especially fun. Away from home at a trunk show, where all my customers would fuss over her, she could be just a normal girl. No one had to know she couldn't do math easily or read maps, or that she had differences of any kind.

DIVVYING THINGS UP

Something very interesting has happened between the girls as they have grown up: they each sort of naturally chose the areas in which they were strongest, and neither would ever trespass on the other's field.

For example, when Charlotte was six and Annie was four, we started taking the girls skiing. I'll be very honest here: I don't like to ski. I wasn't always so honest, though. Poor Tom, I gave him the impression that I loved it, from the beginning of our relationship. I learned to ski in college, more or less as a way to meet guys. I thought it was something you were supposed to like, so I made myself seem enthusiastic about it.

I similarly thought it would be a good thing for Charlotte and Annie to learn. Skiing is a very social sport. And Tom really loves it.

At first, both girls seemed to take to it. They enjoyed their beginner lessons. But as Annie began to advance, Charlotte started to show some resistance.

It didn't help that one very insensitive ski instructor humiliated her by comparing her to Annie and other kids, out loud. They were taking a group lesson, and toward the end, the instructor discussed their levels. He said, of Annie and her friend, "Okay, these two are the best." Of Charlotte he said, somewhat callously, "She's last."

That was the end of skiing for Charlotte. Tom offered several times to help her, one-on-one. She took him up on it once or twice, but then declared herself a nonskier.

I asked her recently whether she remembered what motivated that choice. Was it just that she didn't like skiing? Or was it the distinction between herself and her sister?

"Annie was better," Charlotte stated very simply. "I didn't want to do it because she was much better."

So, Annie got skiing. That's her thing. And she's awfully good at it. Charlotte and I have become expert at *après ski*. As I've mentioned before, we spend the whole time in the lodge, either reading or doing arts projects together.

Annie won't touch art. That's Charlotte's. Annie used to enjoy being creative with Charlotte and me, but somewhere along the line, she gave it up. I recently asked her about that, too. She said, "I let Charlotte have art. I like art, but it's not like I'm repressing some great talent or burning desire. I'd rather let that be Charlotte's area."

It was a mixed blessing, this division of labor—positive in that they don't want to be competitive with one another, and each wants to let the other shine; negative in that they are both confined to one area or another without feeling free to try everything. But, I suppose, it's all part of how we get along.

GETTING ALONG

Even though as a family we really like hanging out with one another, there are always issues that come up, and they're often LD-related, at least to some degree. They especially come up when we've got a lot of free time on our hands, and the more adventuresome among us (read: Tom and Annie) want to do something very active and vigorous. I'd usually be up for the challenge (except, of course, if it's skiing we're talking about).

But often, I'd stay inside or under a tree with Charlotte, while Tom and Annie got active.

Charlotte typically shies away from even trying the things they want to do. When she was very young, she used to love being invited by Tom to join in physical activities—running, ice skating, roller skating, bike riding. His enthusiasm was contagious and delicious. But as she and her sister grew, Charlotte began to want to quit early. Part of the problem was that Annie was naturally better at most of the activities. That would be compounded in time, as Annie would stick with those activities and keep getting better at them, which would make Charlotte even more reluctant to try the next time.

Also, though, Charlotte found many of the activities very difficult, and they required a lot of patience and focus on her part. She doesn't have the stamina to play soccer; she'll play tennis for a few minutes or not at all. Charlotte doesn't have the kind of muscle memory most people do; when she tries certain things for the second, third, or fourth time, it may as well be the very first time, and that brings about anxiety and fear.

The result is that when we want to do something active as a family, we often either split up into two groups of two or try dragging Charlotte along, as she trails us reluctantly and slows everything down.

Often, Charlotte and I have stayed behind when Tom and Annie have gone off to do sports. It's been a mixed blessing for me. There have been times when I would have rather been biking or hitting tennis balls, but I felt Charlotte's need for me and her desire to do quieter activities. So, I would feel a little bit resentful. But other times, I have been glad that Charlotte wanted to stay inside, to read or draw or watch a video with me. This was great bonding time for us. We were able to open up to each other. I was able to understand what she was saying better, especially without feeling the pull of both Annie's and Tom's need for attention.

I also got to realize how nice it is just to "chill," to talk and just be with someone close to you, like your child—really, it's one of the most enjoyable and important aspects of being alive, if you ask me. And, I came to notice that I don't have as much passion for physical activity as Tom does. Hanging back with Charlotte let me off the hook of having to be really active!

IT'S LIKE RIDING A BICYCLE . . .

Other times, though, Charlotte and I would go along with Annie and Tom, often with disastrous results. To be fair to Charlotte, even when she does try and does her best, Annie and Tom, two enthusiastic athletes, still feel she is holding them back. This is especially true when it comes to cycling, something both Tom and Annie take seriously, and something I've come to appreciate and enjoy.

Riding a bicycle has always been a challenge for Charlotte. Learning was especially traumatic for her, more so, I believe, than for most kids. It involved so much coordination of motor functions—feet, hands, vision, balance. Getting her body and mind to do all they needed to do at the same time was a lot to ask of her.

Tom did most of the teaching. Charlotte was six at the time. I can remember watching the two of them, Tom standing out in the driveway in our home on Long Island, encouraging, cajoling, guiding, and Charlotte coming *this close* to learning, but then giving up. It was just that last leap of faith, the letting go, that was so hard for her. She couldn't; she wouldn't. (Interestingly, about two years later, when Annie was learning to ride her two-wheeler and became gung-ho about it, Charlotte suddenly ran to her bike, jumped on and rode off.)

Even after Charlotte learned to ride, biking wasn't her favorite thing to do. It was a source of anxiety for her, and that put her at odds with the rest of us. Getting out of our driveway at our home on Long Island, which has a bit of a slope and runs into the street with a sharp left, has always been daunting for her. When we talked about going for a ride through the neighborhood as a family, just the idea of the driveway would make Charlotte reluctant to agree. We came up with the solution of walking her bike down to the street—one of many cases of mom and Charlotte working out a strategy to suit the situation and allow normal family life to continue.

Once we were riding through the back streets of our neighborhood, Charlotte would be fine and could actually get in the groove, laugh, talk, and look around. But if we had to stop for some reason and then start again, the fun stopped. She'd set the pedals in the right place and survey the road, looking up and back and up and back for any oncoming cars. Sometimes her foot would slip and kick the pedal backwards out of position, and then she'd have to walk the bike forward until it was in the right place again. Then, she'd start again, looking up and back and up and back for the cars. Because she wasn't sure of herself; any car, no matter how far down the road, was cause to stop totally and wait until it had meandered down and past. Charlotte doesn't have the same distraction filters that we have, and she's much more fearful because she's less coordinated. It's always been very hard for the rest of us to have patience with this. But I found that if I spoke calmly and encouragingly—"Take your time, Charlotte . . . that's right"—she could proceed beautifully.

About the time the girls became teenagers, Tom and I took up bicycling as a "thing." Instead of my yard-sale turquoise cruiser (coaster pedals, big handlebar basket—you get the picture), I got a "real" bike for distances with clip-in pedals and padded Lycra shorts. Tom and I began a new tradition of spending ten days each summer bicycling in France, just the two of us. And our Long Island family bike rides took on a different tenor. The girls and I would still meander through our neighborhood streets, but from time to time, we would also go longer distances and take some different roads than Charlotte and Annie had ridden as little girls.

One recent summer Sunday morning, Tom loaded all four bikes into the van, and we drove out toward a beautiful, single-lane beach road in Westhampton. It was a major production, and no speedy task getting everything together: helmets, water bottles, bikes, windbreakers, repair tools, sunglasses, sunscreen, four bikes with tires pumped up, and four individuals ready to go. Usually, preparing for an expedition like this takes about two hours in our family. And once we're all set to go, of course, there are two or three "Oh, wait I forgot something!" returns into the locked house.

It was a beautiful, clear day with flowers in bloom, ideal for a family bike ride. At the beginning, the road was very quiet and ran past some beautiful, huge, shingled houses on one side and a nature preserve on the other. I was in heaven, enjoying the sightseeing, the houses, the landscaping, the gardens, the architecture, the sea grass, the dunes, the gulls, and the sound of the pounding surf. Best of all, there were no cars at that time of day.

Although Charlotte had been hesitant to go on the ride, she opted not to stay at home while Annie, Tom, and I went. It seemed she wanted to be with all of us, so she was willing to leave her comfort zone. Also, she was enthusiastic about our plans to stop at a fried-clam shack for lunch halfway through.

At the beginning, everything was going well. But after about an hour and a half, the beach road ended in a four-lane, busy street and a long, tall bridge over an inlet. Clams awaited on the other side. We started out pedaling as hard as we could to get up momentum, but Charlotte and I ended up walking our bikes over the bridge when it got too steep—the panoramic view and the wind probably made the bridge seem steeper than it was.

After a tasty, deep-fried lunch, we set off on the second half of the ride. Here, the road was not so quiet; there were no sidewalks, and, initially, there was a lot of traffic. Well, Charlotte freaked out. The cars whizzing by scared her. Their presence made her freeze. If we could just get past this section of a mile or so, the road would get quieter, but Charlotte began wobbling and then stopped. Because of her fear, her legs wouldn't get the pedals going in rhythm. She panicked, doubting her ability to make her body do what it needed to do. This is one of the most perplexing and trying aspects of LD: emotions like fear can be literally paralyzing. The body and the mind, which already have difficulty communicating, stop cooperating altogether.

As Charlotte got scared, I got uptight. I was urging; she was trying, failing, then trying again, but this time in an angry and frustrated manner. Then, she gave up. Annie and Tom were already further down the road, looking back at us across the intersection. Everyone was waiting for Charlotte. All of the pressure, of course, made it worse. As Charlotte struggled and struggled, the bike wobbled more and more, and she had less and less control of her body, her bike, and herself. She broke down and cried, "I can't. I want to go home. I don't want to be here."

That was the end of our fun family bike trip. Tom rode back and got the car to pick us all up. I can only imagine how annoyed he must have been. Annie and Tom felt unsatisfied. Charlotte felt at her wit's end. I felt pulled all over the place. Maybe I could have handled it in such a way that everyone would have been happy, perhaps telling Tom, "You and Annie go on ahead and circle back in about twenty minutes," and to Charlotte, "Let's you and I walk our bikes for a while till we come to a quiet spot." We had all day really—just because it "should" have been a four-hour bike ride didn't mean it couldn't be a six-hour bike ride. But I didn't think of that at the time.

The car ride back to the house was uncomfortable. We were all disappointed, confused, angry—and silent, each for different reasons.

I think this sort of incident is often hardest felt by Tom. He just wants to be able to enjoy his scarce free time with his kids—both his kids. He's athletic, and so is Annie, so it's easy for them to bond. But to find common ground with Charlotte, it's just not easy for him. He wonders constantly what activities they might be able to enjoy together.

A BRAND NEW DAY

All hope is not lost, though, for Charlotte and Tom's being able to enjoy time alone together, even to get exercise together. A major shift occurred in the second half of Charlotte's senior year of high school—a near miracle, really—in which she made marked improvements as a runner. Suddenly, she was comfortable going running with Tom and the rest of the family. Not only was she more adept, but she became eager to do it, as well.

Physical exercise has never really been Charlotte's thing, and running was always something she did awkwardly. When she was a very little kid, and running was just part of playing, she did it unself-consciously, but we noticed that she held her right arm bent, with her right shoulder partly raised. Her steps were ungainly; one leg would kick out to the side, and it was as if the steps and the movement of her arms were not in sync. It briefly crossed our minds that maybe there was some sort of neurological misconnection there. This was before she was diagnosed with LD.

Through Charlotte's preteen and teen years, Tom would often invite her to run with him, or with all of us. Half the time, she'd say no; the other half of the time, she'd reluctantly say yes and then complain. Tom, Annie, and I were faster than Charlotte and had more stamina. She felt like she couldn't keep up, and she felt pressured.

So, you can imagine our surprise when she joined the track team at school. Tom, especially, was baffled. If she liked running enough for the track team, why wouldn't she go with him? And if she hated it as much as it looked like she did, why did she join the team?

The winter of Charlotte's senior year, we took the girls on vacation in Cozumel, Mexico. Tom came up with a brilliant plan that would help us all work off our fajitas and piña coladas together: a daily run/walk combo at 8 a.m., before the sun became scorching. Tom designed the run/walk combo as a great family compromise. For Charlotte, exercising with the family became more manageable, as well as more palatable. For the rest of us, it meant we could still enjoy a good workout, even if it was less of an intense burn than we were used to.

Tom was in the lead, setting the pace. He'd carefully time the run parts to make it clear that he wouldn't make us run farther than we'd signed up for. It was like, run, walk, chat. Run, walk, chat. Run, oops, accidentally enjoy it, walk, chat. It was a success. We all felt great, physically and mentally, with all those endorphins floating around in our brains—even Charlotte.

The benefits of Tom's efforts were felt long after our Mexico trip. That spring, Charlotte's coach told her she needed to run over the weekends, and she started to say that she wanted to go with Tom so that she could stay in shape.

So, one day shortly after the college acceptances had come in, Tom asked Charlotte to run with him. For maybe the third time in her life, she readily agreed. Tom later told me that as they started out, Charlotte said he was going too fast. He slowed down—no problem. Then, instead of starting to complain that she was tired, that it was too long—*how much further?*—she silently picked up her pace. And picked it up some more. And some more. No comment from either of them. Tom found himself almost struggling to keep up. And he couldn't believe what he was seeing: instead of seeming awkward and ungainly as she always had before, Charlotte strode evenly, gracefully. They finished the three miles along the river together, in sync, as if they had been running together easily for years.

When Tom came back from the run, he was dumbfounded. He reported the details of the run to me. We were both shocked. Charlotte had been fast, steady, willing, engaged in the run. She had the gait of a gazelle. He was blown away by his daughter's

skill and athletic beauty, as well as by her turned-around atti-
tude—and he told her so. Charlotte seemed surprised, and delighted. The more he went on and on, the more Charlotte
beamed.

That weekend on Long Island, the three of us went for a run.
This time, Charlotte started out completely engaged—in the
zone. She was fast, relaxed, confident. Tom ran alongside me,
and we both watched her easy stride as she ran just up ahead of
us. "Remember how it used to be?" I asked. "Where did this
come from? Look at her ease." I wondered, was it the confidence
she gained from getting into college? Had it been Tom's efforts
to create an exercise plan that included her in a comfortable
way? We may never know.

Tom alternately ran alongside me, and we talked and admired
our beautiful daughter, in control, enjoying, delighting, show-
boating, in an area she had never bothered to pursue. And then
Tom would run up alongside Charlotte, her ponytail bobbing,
lean legs moving easily, leaving me further and further behind,
happy as I've ever been.

Chapter 8

STOP THE INSANITY

THE FEMINISTS OF THE 1970S NEVER WARNED US THAT "having it all" came with a heavy price tag, that in juggling a big career, marriage, and kids, you might never feel like you were doing your best at any of them. They never indicated that the constant ride on the merry-go-round might be exhausting, wear you down emotionally, and bring up conflicting, unflattering feelings.

Of course, to me, all feelings other than joy and optimism were unflattering. I believed for most of my life that I needed to be perfect, to project an image of invincibility and invulnerability, not to mention contented perkiness.

My adult life interfered with that plan. There's no escaping it: adult life is hard. Whether you love or hate your job, are partnered or single, have kids or don't, the realities of being a grown-up are often sobering and difficult to face. Add to that having a child with special needs, and it only gets much harder and more emotionally complicated.

It's appropriate to have some messy feelings when you are going through all that I went through. It's appropriate for *anyone* to have real human feelings and to exhibit them. To quote my daughters in their preteen years, Duh! But that was not for me, I decided a long time ago, probably some time in my adolescent years. I had to hold it together, shoulders up, chin high, smile broad.

Until I couldn't anymore.

A person can only juggle a million difficult things while bottling up her emotions and acting like everything is just fine for so long. That's just the way it is—it's like a physical law of nature. There comes a point where something, or everything, has to give.

For me, that point came in 1998, when I was forty-seven. After years of containing my emotions, suddenly, I just couldn't do it anymore. I physically couldn't.

I am pretty sure that the straw that broke my back was the long pent-up stress of dealing with Charlotte's learning differences. My tumultuous feelings about her LD added that critical bit to my ever-growing, ever-tightening internal knot. I think I might have been able to keep shoving my anxieties about everything else down deep inside if it hadn't been for that.

Charlotte's LD was a difficulty that was in our face. It changed every year and required a lot of administrative energy. What's more, it was a very public expression of human imperfection and vulnerability. I could hide most of my vulnerabilities. Charlotte's could not be hidden. I couldn't act like hers weren't there—nor, eventually, could I pretend mine weren't. I had to deal, not just operationally, but emotionally, not just for my sake, but for hers as well.

At the time, I wasn't very happy about it. But, later, I came to realize that Charlotte had been an example for me, helping me to become "real" and inspiring me to heal.

AN UNEXAMINED LIFE

I had been expert at hiding my emotions not just from everyone around me but from myself, as well. I knew just how to tuck them away as soon as they threatened to come to the surface. The result would be this feeling of a knot in my stomach. Often I could feel it throughout my entire body. For a long time, I knew how to live with that knot. But in 1998, that knot started twisting and turning inside me, wringing me out, begging for me to do something to untie it.

I know exactly when I first noticed my knot. I have a strong visual image of that realization. It was during tenth grade at White Station High School, when I was taking an exam for advanced biology. I never thought of myself as a scientist—I was much more literature oriented—but I had a fantastic, riveting teacher who made me love biology. It opened a whole new world to me.

But the class was very hard, and I was afraid I wouldn't be able to keep up. I remember reading the chapter on the ornithine cycle, the process by which the body converts ammonia into urea. I had to read it and reread it in order to get it. I loved learning about what was going on in our bodies. It was fascinating to me. I wondered what else was going on in there that I hadn't learned about yet. I got a heady, physical feeling of exhilaration from learning this fascinating stuff. But it was also the hardest course I had ever encountered.

I decided that the way to go was to throw myself at it, to learn it systematically, thoroughly, one fact at a time. I remember setting up a fold-away card table by the fireplace in the living room and getting out our Underwood Elite typewriter and going through the textbook chapter by chapter, typing out notes. I had discovered that the process of taking notes was a good way for me to learn and understand difficult matter. I did this all through college and still rely on it today. I guess I had my learning style, just like Charlotte has hers.

Typing notes worked for me. Processing the information through my fingers somehow helped it get into my brain. The textbook was thick and dense, and I went at it this way for hours and hours. I typed and typed, faster and faster, holding my breath, trying to get through the book. It was actually exhilarating: I had a mission, and I had a strategy—all I had to do was marshal my concentration and physical stamina to help me get there. I had to block out all distractions, not think about going outside and goofing off or watching TV—or about anything but this biology. I felt I had to memorize the scientific names, terms, functions, body parts in order to understand the Big Concept. I had to "nail" the details obsessively, and that would lead me to the big picture.

I remember my mother asking me after a while, "Don't you want to take a break? Do you have to work so hard?"

Yes, I had to work that hard, but not just because I liked the subject. More importantly to me, it was the only way I could deal with the knotty feeling at the center of me. It was the physical manifestation of the anxiety I was having over getting through the material and absorbing it in time for the exam. Would I be able to understand it all? Could I cram it in, ram it so hard into my brain that my brain would hold onto it, "get" it? It turns out I could. I got an A on that exam.

I didn't realize that this strategy was really a way of repressing anxiety. The feelings of excitement and newfound maturity masked deeper feelings of anxiety and dread. I wasn't fully aware of this disturbing aspect of my "brilliant" ability to concentrate. When my mother would gently suggest I take a break from my studying, I'd insist, "No thanks, I'm fine." I remember noticing that when I finished for the night and went to bed, this knotty feeling went with me. I was surprised that it lingered after I had left the typewriter and the book. It was very physical. My skin tingled. There was an uncomfortable alertness in the back of my neck, a mild constriction in my chest. I figured it was just general nervousness before an exam that every teen feels.

I didn't realize that this was the beginning of a pattern of chronic anxiety. It was so seductive because, most of the time, it accompanied success. It seemed to come along with high performance, deadlines, competitions. But it was like a computer virus that comes along with something desirable and then takes on a destructive life of its own. A little bit of anxiety can enliven and be an effective motivator. But for me, it became a way of life.

This feeling resurfaced fleetingly in my consciousness from time to time when I was in college. I still didn't know it was a "thing" that had a name. I'd notice it and brush it off. I never identified it as anxiety. In fact, I don't think in my whole life, before turning forty-seven, that I ever thought or said, "I'm feeling anxious." That was something you'd only hear in a Woody Allen movie, and in my mind, it definitely wasn't a sentiment to admire.

I realize now that during my college years, during my early New York years, and during my prime career-building years, I was totally out of touch with myself and had no idea that this was the case. It didn't even occur to me to question what I was feeling. The idea of pausing, looking inside myself, and taking a moment to notice my emotions was absolutely foreign. Such an endeavor seemed to me a waste of time.

HIGH ANXIETY

When I was forty-seven, Charlotte was twelve. She was a "tween," a girl on the verge of teenagerhood. She was shy and awkward and very, very needy of me at that point. She didn't want to socialize much; during weekend downtime, she only wanted to spend quiet time with me. She had difficulty with my busy travel schedule, becoming sad when I would leave on trips.

As for me, I was at the height of my high-powered go-getting at the office. I was working like a fiend, as was everyone else on my staff. It was a bit of a killer environment back then, but I just kept on working and smiling.

The more I had to handle, to juggle, to run—career, travel, family, Charlotte's LD—the more I buried feelings of doubt, vulnerability, and disappointment and, especially, any hint of depression. And the more my internal knot grew, the more I medicated it with hard work, a few evening cocktails, running, scheduling, writing notes, and doing, doing, doing.

Work was drug number one. It was where I went to escape my anxiety. And Charlotte needed me to be away from work more. I felt my wings were clipped by Charlotte's neediness. I've come to realize, though, that that is only part of the story. I also saw my own buried, unacknowledged neediness in hers. And I was anxious about her future. Would she always struggle in life? Would she have friends? Would she be able to live and function on her own some day?

One day that year, I found myself feeling as if I couldn't breathe. I was at home in the evening, and, suddenly, I was hyperalert, my mind and heart both racing. Every muscle in my body was tense. I had no idea what was happening, except I thought I was going to die.

I called Tom and he immediately came home. I asked him to hold me, and he did. This went on for about an hour and then mostly subsided. Afterward, I felt as if I had been to the land of Oz and back. I had been in this mysterious place within myself, and it was not pleasant. It was terrifying.

I mentioned this to a friend of mine at work, and she quickly put a name to it. "You had a panic attack," she said. She recommended a therapist, but, no, thank you very little, I, Dana Buchman, had no need for that sort of help.

I went through the motions of investigating whether something was wrong with my heart. Nothing was. I checked with my gynecologist to see if it was some sort of weird hot flash, and he echoed my friend at work: panic attack—go see a therapist.

No. Not for me. No thanks. To me, psychotherapy seemed whiny and undignified. Of course, I had gone with Annie to a neuropsychologist when she was six, and we weren't getting along. But that was for Annie, right? It was about getting help for my daughter, not me.

Charlotte had been going to a therapist, Dr. Carole Grand, for a long time. Kids with LD need help with particular emotional and social challenges, so that made sense to me. Charlotte went for many years, and in that time, it's amazing how much she grew. With Dr. Grand, she practiced saying what she wanted to say in an understandable way. She also developed the confidence—the conviction, really—that what she was trying to express, even if it didn't come out as smoothly as she'd like, was of value and was worth saying.

This gave Charlotte the chutzpah to insist that people allow her to say what she wanted to say. She learned at our family dinner table to say, "Wait. I haven't finished my thought." Or, "Can we go back to this? I don't feel like you heard me." The whole family benefited from that lesson.

Eventually, I was intrigued enough by Charlotte's progress to give therapy a chance myself.

SHRINKING THE KNOT

I found a therapist, a Dr. Fischer. Wow. Me, Dana Buchman, going to see a shrink. After a lifetime of chuckling at the *New Yorker* cartoons making fun of psychologists, here I was seeking one out.

The first day I walked into his office, I could only think, what if someone sees me? What if someone asks, What are you doing on the Upper East Side at 7:00 a.m.? I'd see myself in cartoon form: uh-oh, there's Dana Buchman *in* the *New Yorker* cartoon! She's actually going to pay quite a lot of money and pour her heart out over a period of time to someone who's going to pretend to listen to her but is really going to be thinking about his squash game. Ha, ha, ha.

But I went, and, suddenly, I was optimistic. I figured it was very simple: I had a problem, and going to the shrink would fix it. He was going to help untangle the knot and make sure I never had another panic attack and that would be that.

Of course, as I would learn there, psychotherapy is a process, often a long process. It's not at all like getting calamine lotion from the pharmacy for poison ivy. This wasn't about simply treating some pesky symptoms—a panic attack and a knot. It would take months, then years, to discover and work through what was causing them—my upbringing, my job, my children, my husband, and, of course, me.

I have kept a few scribbled notes from my sessions over the years. I know that patients notoriously find it difficult to hear what their shrinks (and their own minds) tell them about their psychology. So, I thought writing down difficult epiphanies could help me process them and "get" them, the way I thought typing would help me "get" the ornithine cycle.

It was—is—a long process, eight years and counting. It took five years for me to make significant progress. It's an education that proceeds at a turtle's pace, and in the beginning, that frustrated me, even though I was trying to examine and change forty-seven years' worth of behavior. I'd come away from an all-too-brief, fifty-minute session with Dr. Fischer with some tiny bit of revelation, an epiphany, and then, a few weeks later, have to be reminded of it all over again. In typical Dana fashion, I asked Dr. Fischer if I could just hire him for three days at a time and get to the bottom of it all at once. I'd go in with detailed notes and lists of things I wanted to tackle, get done. I asked him when would I be cured, and he smiled and said, "When you quit coming in here with lists."

TANGLED UP IN BLUE

In my imagination, the knot inside me — the tangle of nerves and emotions that I kept constricting inside myself for years — takes a few different forms. Sometimes, it seems like a dark brown rock, cold, solid, and unforgiving. Other times, it seems like a hard, gnarled growth, such as you might see on diseased oak trees like the ones I grew up with in Memphis. As I started to work things through and became more optimistic, the knot seemed like a dark brown braised onion from which I would peel away layers as part of my journey of self-discovery. There were many layers, a lot to discover about my own psyche.

One of the biggest revelations was a belief I didn't even realize I held, a belief that was the major underpinning of my worldview: that feelings of anger, disappointment, and sadness over anything less grave than death were weak and shameful. I was alive and healthy in a relatively safe country with a great family, so what right had I to feel anything but happy and confident?

Of course, I had those "weak" and "shameful" feelings. I wasn't going to show them to anyone, though. I was terrified that those feelings would drive family, friends, and, above all, Tom, the love of my life, away from me. They wouldn't love me; they'd despise me and abandon me, and I'd die. But what was really killing me was holding in all those emotions.

Somewhere toward the end of my fifth year working with Dr. Fischer, I was able to make some headway against this absurd, sad, lonesome view of life. It was daunting, I must say. The deeper I dug, the more I saw things that, at first, made me think, *Ewww! I'm feeling that? Yuck! How embarrassing! How idiotic! I do that? Oh, man! What a loser!*

I had to get used to looking at these feelings that had been safely locked inside me and then to the idea that it was okay to have feelings like shame and anger and disappointment. It was like taking How to Be Human 101. I didn't know how to tolerate real feelings, other than the discomfort of fighting my feelings, to which I had grown so accustomed. But I soon began to see that I could live a richer, more authentic life rather than having to be a cardboard cutout—a version of me that Tom and I have now come to refer to as "Perky Perky."

PERKY PERKY
HAS LEFT THE BUILDING

I told Dr. Fischer that I noticed that Tom and I were drifting. I wanted so badly to feel close to Tom, especially with all I was experiencing, but something was in the way. Dr. Fischer explained to me that *I* was in the way. By keeping a large part of myself isolated, under wraps, unreachable to my husband, I was contributing to the drifting. He convinced me it would be a good idea to reveal my true feelings to Tom. Instead of driving Tom away, letting him inside would make us closer, Dr. Fischer insisted.

It was strange to me to hear this. I couldn't believe it. I should *tell* Tom when I felt angry? Suppose I had no right to be angry? And I was supposed to do it right on the spot, when I felt it? Not keep it inside, look at it from all sides, calm down for a few days and then, maybe, possibly, bring it up rationally if the occasion arose later in the week? And I was actually supposed to *acknowl-edge* at work when I felt stressed or afraid? I probably spent 50 percent of my energy hiding the fact that I was stressed and afraid!

I was astounded. I had never heard such things before. Suppose Tom thought I was unreasonable and therefore unlovable if I burdened him with my uncomfortable feelings? Suppose my colleagues at work thought I was weak and incompetent?

I was both excited and puzzled by what I was learning. But, for a long time, it didn't make me change the way I operated. I was still going on all engines, running my company, controlling every little detail I could as though my life depended on it, traveling like a fiend, getting up in the middle of the night to get in extra work time.

Eventually, though, something clicked in my brain, and I realized I needed to lighten my load. I wasn't only a designer running her label. I was a wife and a mother, not only of a child with learning differences but of two growing children who needed me. I somehow "got" that I needed to give myself a break, or I would break.

It dawned on me that I needed to delegate some of my work to other, very capable people. I had been micromanaging just about every detail of design for my company, down to reviewing all the buttons. There was no reason someone else couldn't handle some of those details; all that stood in the way was my need to control it all. Lightening my workload to be more available to Charlotte and Annie—and myself—allowed some people on my staff to fulfill their potential and shine in a way they hadn't been able to before.

THANKS FOR SHARING

I wanted to share all that I was learning with Tom. But it was difficult. Shrink visits are organic things—a lot goes on in each session and over the weeks ideas emerge and get partly processed
and submerge only to come up again months later. It's not like I
baked a tray of cookies and could come home and say, "Look
what I've made. Here they are."

I just couldn't give a clear picture of all that I was discovering.
It was also a bit jarring for him to suddenly see me with my "disturbing" emotions revealed, rather than stowed carefully be-
neath my seat. The gradual emergence of a woman who wanted
to put her feelings out there threatened to rock our applecart. I
was struggling with the emergence of my true self. Tom was loving and supportive of my quest as I pursued it, but he didn't
really want a play-by-play report. And I think, sometimes, when
I'd come home from work all roiled up and fit to be tied, he'd secretly long for the Perky Perky girl he married.

Fortunately, we both realized that person wasn't real, and I
couldn't go back to playing her. The quantity of bottled emotions was just too big to stay crammed inside my heart anymore.
Tom was willing to go with me to the new place and help me get
there.

With that settled, I got up the courage to ask him to go with
me to couples therapy. I wanted us to go so we could get reac-
quainted. I still loved the man and he loved me, but over the
years of careers, children, and Charlotte's LD, we had grown
apart. Our tendency toward silence when something was bothering us had become an entrenched habit that we needed to break.

And although we never fought, quite a few hot buttons had built up over the years. Little things that we never processed had accumulated. I've seen it happen in tons of couples: that Tom didn't pick up his shoes drove me around the bend. That I didn't put the top securely on the pot with boiling vegetables made him nuts. And then there were bigger things that we didn't share with each other: I was perpetually worried that the next season of clothing wouldn't sell at retail. He'd sometimes worry about catastrophic illness. And then, of course, there were our fears about Charlotte and her learning differences and how they would continue to affect her life.

So, Tom and I went to couples therapy. Loren, this handsome, gray-haired man on the Upper West Side, came into our lives. Loren is a Southerner, an ordained minister, and a poet. He's also an athlete and a "man's man," so he offered something for each of us. We later learned that he also has learning differences, which gave us a great new perspective on LD. If this great couples therapist had it, it couldn't be the end of the world. He has been a wonderful, inspiring coach for us in many ways.

But it was so hard at first. Just getting there after a long day at work was difficult, each time overcoming the embarrassment of walking into his office, nodding and mumbling excuses when we'd bump into people we knew—why were we so far from our own neighborhood? And the work itself was hard. Loren started by helping us relearn how to listen to each other. We had to go through maddeningly difficult exercises like, "Tom, tell Dana how you felt after such and such an incident." "Dana, what did you hear him say?" "Tom, did she get it? And is there more?" "Dana, now what did Tom say now?" "Has she got it, Tom?" Ok, ok. I know. It sounds *so* silly. But it is a staggering challenge after a conflict to put aside your own point of view and state fully and clearly what the other person perceived and felt. It is nearly impossible not to add your own gloss ("Loren, he said he felt mad but he had no right to because I didn't do anything" turns out not to be an acceptable answer!).

We were learning, for the first time, to really listen to each other. Thich Nhat Hanh, the Vietnamese Buddhist monk and writer, calls it "deep listening." It's temporarily suspending your own point of view and not interrupting to concentrate only on the other's words and intentions. Ironically, this attentive way of listening was something Charlotte, with her disorganized speech and faltering phrasing, had needed from us all her life.

In time, Tom and I both got the hang of identifying feelings, learning not to run away in terror from them, and expressing them.

Eventually, family matters started to come up in our sessions—the complexity of having kids. It wasn't long before we got to the subject of Charlotte's LD and its impact on all of us.

Tom and I both finally acknowledged how we weren't comfortable talking about LD to each other or to the girls. It became clear, as it had in the other areas of my life, that not talking about LD was more destructive than the uncomfortable feelings that would emerge from bringing it up. Tom and I started to make ourselves point to that big, pink elephant in the room and acknowledge the difficulties it was bringing to the family. We recognized that if we could talk about it easily in the family, the distress of knowing but not saying would diminish for all four of us.

With the credibility of first-hand experience with LD, Loren encouraged us to name it, to acknowledge its power, to express our frustration and disappointment with it. That, he said, would set us free.

GOOD RESULTS

Together, my individual therapy with Dr. Fischer and the couples therapy with Tom have helped me to make great strides. I am less fearful of telling Tom, the girls, and my colleagues how I feel, although I've still got a long way to go. I'm still working it through. I've realized that telling Tom, my sweet husband, when I am distressed, embarrassed, afraid, sad, or disappointed doesn't drive him away. It really does bring us closer. It turns out that the real me is not less desirable than my Perky Perky persona, that false, impossibly Enthusiastic Happy Wonder Woman.

Charlotte and Annie have both been willing partners with me in this quest. I remember one evening, we were sitting at the dinner table, and I had had the epiphany that I just had to spit my feelings out, quit editing myself all the time. I wanted to try to let it all hang out so I could get used to a flow of feelings without sending them inside for storage, where they'd get added to that knot. Tom helped me clue the girls in to this resolution.

"Girls, Mom has something to tell you," he said.

I saw fear and horror and apprehension sweep over their faces.

I rushed to say, "I'm going to try to express my feelings as they come up."

Annie burst into tears, and Charlotte teared up.

"That's all?" one of them asked.

"We thought you were getting a divorce!" said the other.

"Sure, Mom, express your feelings!"

They were relieved—and supporting me fully.

Suddenly, I didn't have to be fake anymore. By the way, I hadn't been a *complete* fake — there is a part of me that is sort of perky and optimistic. I really do believe that most things can be handled and worked out. But I'm not only perky — I'm also sometimes a puddle of fears and angry frustration and disappointment and sadness. Now I was free to turn off my internal censor. I didn't have to censor myself in my marriage. I didn't have to hold in what was bothering me. If I shared myself with my family, I could get their help and feel their love.

Charlotte, in particular, has been a good partner for me in this quest to face the imperfect, unlovely parts of myself. I felt her love flood over me. She knew all about showing feelings that made her appear weak and vulnerable. Not by choice, she lived her life that way. And she was more comfortable with her weakness than I was with mine. When I'd call from the kitchen in a fury, "OK, I just told everyone dinner is on, and no one is coming to sit down, and that makes me angry!" she'd come in laughing and say, "Go, Mom! Express your feelings!"

SELF-MEDICATING

After a few years of individual and couples therapy, I realized I had to take another big step: giving up alcohol.

It started in January of 2003, when Tom suggested we try to go a month without drinking, just to give our livers a rest after the holidays. At first I thought, *Okay, sure.* We'd done that before. Then, I strained and struggled through that month with great difficulty and realized I was dependent on my two gin and tonics in the evening. Now, we're not talking about someone who was getting drunk, or even sloppy. It was very civilized. At the end of a long workday, my two gin and tonics would buy me an hour or two of less stress.

Growing up, when my parents had dinner parties, they always began with "highballs" in the living room. During the week, they always had one beer before dinner, usually out on the terrace in the Memphis early evening heat. They never, ever drank to excess. Rather, it was part of civilized adult life.

I fell in love with Tanqueray and tonic when I was in college. Like about five hundred million teens before me, I felt drinking looked grown up, modern, that it was romantic in some way—gin and tonics seemed Southern, part of my roots. Having a "signature" drink—always gin and tonic—could become part of my identity. Plus, my favorite Brown professor, the man who inspired in me my lifelong love of nineteenth-century literature, drank with gusto. When I went to his house to baby-sit, he would offer me a drink. Though I can clearly see the inappropriateness now of drinking while caring for someone else's kids, at the time I didn't want to disappoint him in anything.

During my early years in New York, I kept up the gin and tonics. During the week, it was usually a couple of them after work, followed by wine with dinner. On weekends, I'm sorry to say, it was sometimes to excess. I had a hangover at least one day of every weekend. During the 1970s, downtown Manhattan social life centered on loft parties. You'd hear about them through friends of friends of friends. There were usually about one to two hundred people there, depending on the loft space, all cool and groovy pioneers who were fixing up and living in old warehouse buildings downtown. I also went to the Mudd Club, a signless, grungy, wild dance club in a back alley that was the height of "in" for those Tribeca dwellers who rejected Studio 54, which was raging in midtown. My weekend partying, with its accompanying overdrinking, felt like a continuation of college youthful wildness. It was part of being young and cool in New York.

In the early 1980s, my social life changed. A typical weekend night was spent having dinner with friends or going to the movies—no wild dance clubs. My career had heated up. I was working hard, harder, hardest, traveling to Asia six, seven, eight times a year, and one year, even nine times. The adrenaline level in my body was constantly off the charts. Alcohol smoothes out the edges. It dulls the effects of the adrenaline. The adrenaline coursing through my body was what allowed me to work that hard. The alcohol would buy me a few hours of relaxation in the evening until the adrenaline woke me up in the middle of the night to start working, worrying, planning, spinning all over again. My main source of relaxation was alcohol. Its presence in my life became almost a ritual signpost to mark the end of the workday and the beginning of "free" time.

The harder I worked, the more I associated alcohol with relaxation, with chilling out, hanging out. There were two Dana's: the way I was and felt at work—highly focused, missing nothing, laser vision, painfully intense, high adrenaline, like an animal in a state of emergency—and the way I felt at home and with friends—with all that intensity chemically mellowed by alcohol.

I was careful never to drink to excess during the week. The weekends were a different story. Although I wasn't partying at clubs, I drank more on the weekends than during the week. When I thought about how much I was drinking, I looked on it as part of the fast-paced, glamorous life of a jet-set designer that I was leading—the work hard/party hard continuum. I was proud of my body's ability to take all this without a protest (very important)—I was high on intensity—bring it on. Never say you can't do something, never cry uncle, never say it's too much. In fact, add to the challenge with bravado.

When I married Tom in 1985, I was still living the hectic life of a young designer. Alcohol seemed necessary then, and even more so when we had the girls, and when I began dealing with Charlotte's learning differences. There was so much intensity. The alcohol was a part of what allowed me to keep it up, to sustain it. I was overwhelmed and didn't know it, wouldn't admit it. Alcohol, along with my tremendous self-discipline and the wondrous powers of psychological denial, enabled me to remain oblivious to the unsustainability of my way of living.

I didn't consider myself an alcoholic. After all, I wasn't consuming *that much*. I had been able to quit drinking totally and effortlessly when I was pregnant and nursing both girls—almost four years total. I never binged and never drank more than my "limit" during the week. But it was consistent, night in, night out.

The adrenaline/alcohol cocktail was part and parcel of my normal state of being. It was only later that I began to realize that my relationship to alcohol was that of an alcoholic.

Years later, when I was around forty, I began to realize that drinking means different things to different people. I got a call from St. Vincent's Hospital. My dear, older brother Jim, a sculptor who lived in a loft a couple of blocks away in Tribeca with his wife and young daughter and who was a diabetic, had collapsed and was in the emergency room. It soon emerged that he had congestive heart failure. And then, it emerged that it was brought on by drinking.

I had had no idea. Jim was an alcoholic and had been for years. His doctor told him if he didn't quit drinking he would die. I started investigating Hazelden intervention procedures so his loved ones could surround him and make him quit. But he beat us to the punch. He just quit. Just like that. Cold turkey. With the help of Alcoholics Anonymous (AA), done.

A few months later, he and I talked and realized that there was alcoholism on both sides of our family. We'd known about some, found out about more. It had never been something I thought of as having to do with my immediate family. But, of course, there is a genetic component, and we were prime candidates.

I adored Jim and still do. My family has very tight bonds. Jim and his family lived down the street from us, and we'd have brunch most weekends. But I realized later that we never really talked. As part of Jim's journey with AA, he learned that a component of the therapy is learning to open up with family and friends so that you can get closer. Well, the more he opened up, the closer I felt, and the more I loved him. I realized that there was more to know of him and that ours was a much richer relationship without his alcohol between us. I wanted this openness, this richness, in my family life, too.

By the time I gave up drinking, I had been in therapy for five years. I was much more attuned to what was going on in my mind, body, and psychology than I had been in the 1980s and 1990s.

When I began my month of no drinking, I noticed how I felt. I remember one night walking up the street after a typically intense day at work, knowing that I wouldn't have a drink when I got in. And it scared me. With no drink, I'd have to calm down my intense, frantic work self and look carefree and relaxed all on my own. I was panic stricken; I realized that my body prickled all over, and I had a sense of dread and "No-o-o-oh!" Wow. All this physical and emotional need, this longing desperation. I had no idea I needed the drinks so much. I'm sure I knew on *some* level. I mean, if we were going to a party where the hostess might not have Tanqueray, I often brought my own tasteful bottle. But I never *knew*.

I resolved that the pain of stopping drinking just for a month was so terrible that I didn't ever want to face it again. So, I decided to quit cold turkey. Just like Jim had. He had become an even warmer, more available person. So, maybe I would, too. Rather than medicate my anxiety and my sense of being knotted and overwhelmed, I would take one more step to set it free.

Chapter 9

TEEN SCENE

SO, I WENT INTO THERAPY, STOPPED DRINKING, AND became such a great mom that Charlotte got all better, and we all lived happily ever after. The end.

As if.

Looking inside myself, getting an education into my own psychology, has been one of the best things I have ever done, for myself and for my family. But just because I went to a psychotherapist doesn't mean my uncomfortable feelings went away or that dealing with LD suddenly became easy.

I believe that as a result of therapy, I am better equipped to handle the LD factor and more helpful to Charlotte. But new hurdles just keep on coming. Every year, as Charlotte evolves, so do her issues, relative to where she is in her life. Adolescence brought a whole new set of obstacles, LD related and otherwise.

OUT OF SYNC

All teens and their moms have issues. It's just a law of nature. But with LD in the picture, some of the issues can be magnified.

One of the causes of friction between Charlotte and me—not only when she became a teen but since she was little, too—has been a difference in our energy levels and the way we pace ourselves. I'm not just talking about physical pace, as was evident in bike riding, but psychological pace; I am high energy and very fast moving, and I have never liked to be slowed down.

When I was in high school, my mother accused me of always being "on the go," "on the big wheel" as she used to say. I was involved in everything—school, church, athletic, and social activities—all of which would take me out of the house as many afternoons as I could manage. To me, in those years, being "on the go" seemed the very goal of life. I couldn't sign up for enough social engagements or obligations.

Charlotte, on the other hand, moves slowly. I'm sure part of it is her different wiring, and I suspect part of it is just her personal nature. She's a dreamy, easy-going, relaxed person. She has always liked to be still, to sit alone and draw, or, once she developed the skill, to read. She got involved in some extracurricular activities but mostly preferred to come home after school and just recover from the difficulty of getting through her day.

This clash in our natures was a big problem for me early on, when Charlotte was small. When I would walk with her to the subway to get to an appointment, I would walk really fast. From the time she was little, Charlotte would say to me, "Why are you rushing? We don't have to hurry. I don't like to rush. Can we slow down?" For so many years, when she was small and I was big, I would ignore her requests and pull her along, simply saying "Come on, let's just get there."

But then, when I was in my late forties and beginning to feel overwhelmed with all that I was trying to achieve, something changed in me. I was ready to hear her words. Why *did* we always have to rush or move at a brisk New York City pace? I was ready to learn from her, and I did.

Even though Charlotte's perspective started to make sense to me, I can't tell you how hard it was for me to learn to walk down the street approaching a pedestrian street sign that was flashing and changing from "Walk" to "Don't Walk" without running to make it across the intersection. It took all my willpower not to fly down the subway steps when I heard the train coming, not to rush full speed to make the elevator that was closing rather than wait for the next one.

But Charlotte had mastered this. She always trusts that there will be another train, another elevator car, that the street sign will turn back to "Walk" before too long.

BUDDHA OR WALLFLOWER?

Charlotte's relaxed pace clashed not only with my fast-moving nature but with Tom and Annie's as well. As I've discussed earlier, their athletic drive and Charlotte's resistance to it was a constant conflict to be reckoned with. On weekends, Tom, Annie, and I would look to book up our time with activities and athletics, while Charlotte would want to just kind of hang out. We all agreed that Saturday and Sunday mornings should start out very relaxed, with coffee, pancakes, the *New York Times*, and music. But as the day went on, the rest of us went into high gear while

Charlotte wanted to go into maximal chill. She was happy just to hang out in her pajamas and sit and chat and draw and flip through some books.

On the one hand, after I went through my "midlife crisis" and Charlotte reached high school, I came to see her approach as very positive—exemplary, actually. Charlotte didn't run herself ragged, packing in events and things the way I did. She didn't rush to go outside and run errands and see the latest movie and meet with friends and leave herself no time to think or just be. She knew how sweet it was to live in the present moment instead of always looking around the corner for the next thing to do or become. I was affected by this. I started to slow down a bit on the weekends, planning less. The more I slowed down, the more I enjoyed just being. When I wasn't trying to pack in an absurd amount of work and other activities, Charlotte's slow-moving nature didn't seem as much a disability as a gift, a talent for being in the present and being calm. I have come to rely on Charlotte's calmness, her in-the-moment-ness, to help me slow down and just be. How lucky I have been.

On the other hand, I became concerned that Charlotte didn't have enough of a social life. Why wasn't she part of a big group of friends? Why wasn't she having sleepovers? Why wasn't she on the phone all the time gossiping with girlfriends, begging to stay out past curfew? In tenth and eleventh grades, she would go for months without seeing any kids outside school. She was sociable in school—she wouldn't just sit in the corner and eat by herself—but she never wanted to spend the night out or bring a friend to our house.

I know that kids with learning differences typically have social issues. They are especially self-conscious, afraid that their inabilities and vulnerabilities will be revealed, so many of them keep to themselves. In their teen years, this self-consciousness can be heightened by all the factors that make lots of "normal" teens quiet and shy. There's no end to the list of causes of insecurity and self-doubt during those years.

In Charlotte's case, I think she shied away from groups of kids because she was afraid that she wouldn't be able to keep up with their fast-paced talking and gossiping and teasing, even though her peers also had LD issues. They all had different learning differences and didn't all share the language difficulty that makes it hard for her to track and respond to conversation that is fast paced and packed with nuance. That difficulty has plagued her at parties we have had and dinners with the extended family. Getting her thoughts together in time to say them before the topic changes has always been a major challenge for her. With kids in the lunchroom at school, where the pace is lightning fast, it would be even harder. She was worried about making a fool of herself, saying something stupid, and not being accepted.

This came to my attention in a big way during Charlotte's senior year in high school. One night, my two nieces, Lallie and Petra, both in their twenties, came over. Chatting that evening, we all decided to book a spring vacation trip for Charlotte and her two cousins to celebrate Charlotte's senior year.

At first, Charlotte seemed elated: her first trip alone with "peers"—no adult authority, just three girls going together on a long weekend to Florida. But after Lallie and Petra left, and the initial blush of excitement had faded, Charlotte looked gloomy. My first response was to feel angry at her and then, as I've explained, guilty and frustrated too, that trilogy of emotion. Here we were offering an idyllic getaway weekend with two relatives, cousins whom Charlotte likes. This was a treat that others would be lucky to have. What was there to complain about in this, for Pete's sake? I asked Charlotte, "What's wrong?"

She said, "I don't want to tell you. You'll get mad."

"Try me," I said.

Charlotte took a moment and then answered, "I'm afraid I won't get enough attention."

I lost it. "Not enough attention? Two cousins who love you and are good listeners whom you can spend four days gabbing with? What do you mean you won't get enough attention?"

Charlotte said, "I told you I didn't want to tell you because you'd get mad." She got me there.

With some real effort, I calmed down and put on my "listening hat," as Miss Ding Dong used to say in her 1950s TV show. As we talked, I found out that Charlotte was okay with one cousin going with her, but with two, she was afraid she wouldn't be able to stay in the conversation. Not that Lallie and Petra would deliberately leave her out; they're not like that. But Charlotte had realized from our dinner and exuberant planning session that evening that, in a group conversation, it is hard for her to stay in the game. As group conversation meanders from topic to topic, she might formulate something to say, but if she doesn't get it in at just the right moment, the conversation might flow on to another topic.

We have all had this experience: you lose your chance to make your point and then have to work up another point to interject when the time's right. For Charlotte this is extremely hard. Sometimes, even when she does get the floor, she won't be able to articulate her point quickly, someone may interject, and her train of thought will be broken and then lost. Thinking back,

I realized she hadn't said much at dinner that night in the big group and that, in big groups, she usually doesn't. I could imagine how frustrating that must be, day after day. She has the thoughts, she just often lacks the language skills to spit them out in time to participate in most routine, breakneck-speed group conversations. And this can have profound social consequences. Not life-threatening. Not tragic. But far-reaching.

On one level, I had known that Charlotte had this difficulty and that it affected her social interactions. And I'm sure she has known this for a long time. But that evening, in the spring of her eighteenth year, was the first time we had talked about it directly, straight on. It was saddening and liberating at the same time. We were chipping away, naming the disturbing, far-reaching, unexpected consequences of LD.

HOW TO BE A GIRL 101

That spring I realized that in Charlotte's last six months before college, I needed to coach her to work around the social consequences of her LD. And my support needed to consist of encouragement, admiration, love, and a little pushing. I needed to encourage her to start interacting with other kids more and diving into group conversations. Just as practicing embroidery had strengthened her coordination, practicing conversation would strengthen her verbal abilities. It would also be good for her to get in the habit of taking social chances, learning that it's not such a big deal if people don't always respond the way you want them to.

I got the feeling that at school, even at the Churchill School where there were only thirty kids in her whole grade, Charlotte was avoiding groups of kids, especially the popular, most socially advanced kids. I could picture her putting her beautiful head down, averting her magnificent, deep brown eyes, and appearing as if she were deeply involved in something taking place on the ground so she wouldn't have to attempt talking to others.

One morning on the way to school in a taxi—a rare treat—we had a chance to talk about all this.

That morning I was able to come at Charlotte's social anxiety by addressing my own social anxiety about an upcoming cocktail party put on by the Council of Fashion Designers of America (CFDA), a group whose roster includes just about everyone who's important in my field. I told Charlotte I dreaded this party because I didn't know what to talk about. I was intimidated by the group, I told her. They all seemed so confident, so sure of themselves. Even though my business was bigger than most, even though my label had been around nearly twenty years, even though I had been around the world countless times, had been to parties in London, Paris, Florence, even at the White House, I felt shy about going to this annual event. All I could think about when I went to that party each year was how much I wanted to get home to the girls and Tom. But I realized a big chunk of this longing to be with my family was really a longing to avoid a social situation that was scaring me. I'd rather do just about anything than force my coiffed, made-up, dressed-up, high-heeled self to trot into that chichi venue and try to seem at home and confident and like I ruled the world.

I was dreading it even though I spent my life appearing self-reliant, in control, together, unfazed. What was different about this event was that it called for a type of "perfection" I was not accustomed to mimicking. This group didn't seem to be about being erudite, well read, warm, humane, honest. I felt this group was about gloss, about knowing the right editors and going to the right events, and about self-promotion—all areas I didn't feel competent in at all. I felt that they were all *Fabulous!* at talking about how *Fabulous!* they were, and if I didn't do that also, well then, that would mean I wasn't *Fabulous!* too.

As I talked, something interesting happened: I had thought I started this conversation for Charlotte's benefit, but as I went on, I realized that I had always had a degree of social anxiety myself. It wasn't just about going to the CFDA event. It took trying to help Charlotte with her anxiety for me to see it in myself. I was advising both of us.

I asked Charlotte what her social fear felt like. Being Charlotte, she was so creative and articulate: she said, "It's like there are two Charlottes. Sometimes I can go right up to a group and flirt and joke and put myself out there. I dive in, and when I do, it works, and I have fun, and it's great. But there's another Charlotte who just wants to stay in my room and hide under the covers [don't we all know that feeling!] and stay there all day in the dark in my comfy bed."

I asked her which Charlotte she was feeling like right then. She laughed and looked out the window. "The one who wants to stay at home."

I said, "Just leave that Charlotte at home today. Let out the other Charlotte, the wild Charlotte, the bold Charlotte, Charlotte unhinged."

We both got into that, personifying the fear. We decided to call the scared Charlotte "Sadie." She would just leave Sadie at home (and I would leave Perky Perky there, too). It was actually very useful to separate this fearful persona, name her, and joke about her.

By the time we arrived at our destination, we each had a plan for our day. Charlotte was going to school with the intention of diving in, and I was going to my party with the knowledge that every designer there was human, that I didn't have to appear disguised as what I thought they admired.

When we compared notes that night, it was a happy ending to the day.

I had gone into the party without any fake smiles. Perky Perky had stayed at home, just as I had asked her to. I had not attempted to talk about how *Fabulous!* I was; I had talked about what mattered to me. I ended up having conversations about poetry, about death, and about what one truly felt going into parties like this. I was not afraid to let people see what was really going on in my head. I wasn't afraid they wouldn't think I was successful if I didn't get in that I'd been bicycling in the South of France and that I'd just renovated my wonderful Tribeca loft and my beach home in a très chic village on Long Island. I was astounded that people responded in kind, talking to me in a very real way as well. They'd rather talk about real things too! Out of fear, I had been selling myself and my professional peers short.

Ironically, a great photo of me from that party ran in the *New York Times*, and I didn't mind that it made me feel *Fabulous!*

That day, Sadie behaved and stayed at home, too. Charlotte reported that she had joked with the hottest guy in the school (i.e., joked back rather than putting her head down when he joked with her). She'd gone up to various groups and kids she doesn't usually open herself up to throughout the day and said,

"Hey. What's going on?" which is the universal teen sign of making contact. And, wonder of wonders, not once did any of them say, "You have two heads. We'd never talk to you." They'd responded and chatted and joked.

Throughout Charlotte's senior year, she worked on leaving Sadie home whenever she could, and I worked on banishing Perky Perky to her room, too. We both found that the more we engaged with people, the less afraid of engaging we became. And the more relaxed and authentic we were, the less uptight and fake people were with us. Once again, Charlotte's learning differences dovetailed with mine. Working it through for her helped me work it through for me.

HOW TO TALK TO BOYS 101

Charlotte has the body of a goddess. She's slim and shapely with thick brown hair and warm brown eyes. In recent years, she's preferred to wear her funky, off-beat clothes tight. It's all sexy and curve-hugging. But it wasn't like that when she started high school.

Back then, she wouldn't comb her hair and would layer over her Venuslike shape a big old shapeless *schmatta* (that's Garment Center speak—Yiddish, actually, for "rag"). She'd ball her messy hair back in a childish ponytail (not the studiedly messy pony that the faster girls were wearing). She was incredibly shy around boys and afraid to attract them.

It takes most of us a long time to be comfortable in our bodies and with the way boys respond to us. But for Charlotte, there were so many other insecurities in the way as well. They all conspired to make her self-conscious about everything, even her very attractive looks. Annie, who is equally beautiful and shapely, never struggled in this way.

When Charlotte was in eleventh and twelfth grade, I started saying, "You're beautiful, smart, and sexy. Don't hide." I noticed that on the street, if we passed a handsome boy, she'd immediately look at the ground and pick up her pace. The good news was that she noticed the boy. But the bad news was that she was terrified.

One day during Charlotte's senior year, I tried to nudge her past her fears. My brother was getting married at our loft. His fiancée had two sons from her first marriage who were near the girls' ages, and they came to dinner at our house. I looked up and noticed Annie and Charlotte in a back corner together looking at photos we had just had developed, while the two boys were in another part of the apartment. I went back and said to them both, "No, no, no—get out there."

Later, Charlotte floated back to the kitchen and said, "I'm so shy. I don't know what to say."

I shoved a basket of pita and dip at her and said, "Here, pass these. Get out there."

Later, at dinner, I heard Charlotte diving in at her end of the table, asking the older boy what kind of movies he liked, how he picked his college, who his favorite musician was. I knew it was hard work for her, really hard work. But it sounded very natural and engaging, and the conversation flowed easily! Who said anything about an expressive language disorder?

Eventually, Charlotte got to be a little more comfortable with the whole idea of talking to boys and even dating them. The first thing that changed was her clothing—she is a designer's daughter, after all. The oversized layer came off; the hair became a sensual cascade of waves tumbling across one side of her face, sometimes being shaken out in the sunlight. Instead of looking down, she'd look straight in the eye of the boys she'd run into— short glances at first, but gradually steadier and longer.

And like most things, the more success she had, the more she realized boys would respond to her, the more she'd open up and try. She's still her own person, thoughtful, by no means a "fast girl," I'm proud to say. She doesn't look for self-confidence by throwing herself at boys, but she's starting to feel the power of her beauty and demeanor.

BEING THERE

In her high school years, Charlotte didn't need me only for social coaching; she needed me to coach her academically, to boost her self-esteem in that area.

Prior to that, I hadn't been very involved with Charlotte's schoolwork. After I started therapy and began putting things in perspective—work, Charlotte's LD—I made myself more available.

I began to work closely with Charlotte's teachers. I knew I wasn't supposed to help Charlotte with her specific homework assignments, that it's traumatic for kids with LD to have to show their parents how difficult the work can be for them, but I wanted to be on her team and give her guidance.

Writing assignments were particularly challenging for Charlotte. One of her teachers suggested that when Charlotte had to write a report or essay, I should get her to "free-write" first, to jot randomly everything that came into her head, without thinking about punctuation, relevance, or "correctness" of any kind.

Free-writing for Charlotte comes easily and is something she has always enjoyed. She finds it liberating to say to the computer—that silent, patient, dedicated "listener"—what she sometimes finds hard to express in conversation with friends or family members who tend to rush her to make her point. When I read the free writes, I suspend my urge to correct or say "Huh?" and just read, let the words flow over me, and I get clearly what she is trying to say. With the free-written draft on paper, Charlotte could better start to organize her thoughts and rewrite the report.

Another strategy I learned from one of Charlotte's teachers, one that worked for Charlotte in the same way that free-writing does, was to get her to talk her ideas out first. That one came in handy during the Thanksgiving holiday of Charlotte's senior year of high school, when she had to do a book report on *The Joy Luck Club*, a book she had really enjoyed but that is rich and layered and hard to sum up.

Of course, she waited until Sunday afternoon to begin (what teen doesn't—I know I did). Then, when she thought about doing it, she got overwhelmed. "I don't know how to do this," she moaned. That sense of self-doubt may very well have been behind her putting her homework off.

I asked her what the assignment was. She said she had to write about three of the characters, analyzing them. She kept insisting she didn't know how.

I asked her, "So, what are those characters like? Sit here and tell me about them."

She sat on the sofa next to me, and we cuddled and talked about them. Sometimes she got off into describing the plot line too much ("and then she did this and then that"), but one of

Charlotte's strengths is her ability to read people, and within her chatter, I heard lots of excellent observations about the characters' motivations, their inner lives, their illusions. She felt good after she had talked it through informally, comfortably slumped on the sofa, and without the pressure of sitting in front of the computer's blank screen. She was relaxed and confident that, in fact, she did have something to say. The ideas flowed, and, suddenly, she was able to go to the computer and write her report, without fear and anxiety.

We had a similarly positive experience when it was time for Charlotte to work on her college essays. At first, I dreaded it as much as she did. But I also had a little twinge of anticipation, excitement.

Since it had been many years since I'd written a college essay, instead of diving right in with Charlotte, I actually paused. I tried to think about why I was dreading the process, about what would be hardest for her, and to imagine what frustrations might come up for both of us. I knew Charlotte would get overwhelmed at the size and significance of the project and would have a hard time starting. I knew that she could go to town writing but would again get paralyzed when it came time to edit. I knew that whatever final draft we came to would be full of typos, incorrect grammar, sentence fragments. It would be hard for me not to take over and rewrite the whole essay. Then, I took a moment to imagine if there would be any way to make it a positive, pleasurable experience.

If I could give Charlotte confidence as she approached it, help tease out her wonderful ideas and unleash her wacky stream-of-consciousness writing style, I knew she could have fun expressing herself. If I decided at the beginning that these would be Charlotte's college essays and not mine (I kid you not—I had to go through the thought process to make that clear to myself), then I could let her do them in her way.

Charlotte, Tom, and I were all equally interested in seeing Charlotte get into a college that would understand her learning style and the way she expressed herself and be happy to have her as she was. We realized that it was crucial that Tom and I not apply to those schools, that, instead, Charlotte should.

I had a plan (I love a plan!). I discussed it with Charlotte, and she liked the plan, too.

So, about three or four weeks before the essays were due, Charlotte started writing. I was the parental captain spearheading the college application process, keeping Tom updated with short sentences at dinner that things were going well. I didn't clue him into the exact strategy I'd come up with; the whole project made all three of us so nervous that we didn't bring it up with each other unless it was unavoidable.

The process was time-consuming but amazingly fulfilling and successful. Charlotte is always bursting with ideas and has a quirky, imaginative, evocative style full of quirky metaphors and unusual juxtapositions. I had a blast watching the essays bloom. Like so many kids her age, she worked for hours and hours on them. She would free-write, then put her work aside. Then, she'd reread and correct, reread and correct. She made many thick pencil scratchouts and balloons. Sometimes the marks got so thick that the words themselves disappeared. Sometimes she'd have to go back to an earlier draft because in places the constant revising and effort to organize would strip a passage of its punch and meaning. Like many LD kids, she found that by reading out loud, she could catch lots of errors in her writing; her ears would help her correct mistakes that her eyes couldn't see.

I had decided that my job was to stay with her through the process, to sit on the couch and listen while she read and reread her writing out loud, to encourage and cajole until she came out with an essay that was understandable, if not perfect. I was not going to correct the writing itself. I didn't rewrite any fuzzy phrases, and I didn't proofread—the spelling mistakes and grammar idiosyncrasies all stayed in. I wanted it to be clear for both of us that when Charlotte sent in her applications, they were all hers, that if she was accepted to a college, it would be because of the work she did, not that we did. I also wanted the college to be aware of Charlotte's writing skills as they were so that they could decide if she would meet their standards.

After four or five days and the fifth complete revision, we both thought it was ready. She felt good, and I felt good. Charlotte proudly asked Tom to look at it.

What I forgot to do was to clue Tom into the process. I made a big mistake by not telling him that I was going with the idea that a stream-of-consciousness essay with lots of typos was a valid submission and the way to go with these essays.

Tom must have thought I was crazy when he saw the final draft. I can imagine him giving a puzzled look to himself, shrugging internally. He dutifully took the essay and, with a red pen, promptly highlighted all the typos, misspellings, incomplete sentences, and other imperfections. The paper came back to Charlotte with squiggles all over it! Her face fell.

This, ladies and gentlemen, is the consequence of rushed lives and an example of how important it is for parents to be on the same page with one another in managing LD. As far as Tom knew, he was doing a loving thing; he had a pen in his hand, and he did what he knew to do with it. "How would I have known?" he asked me when I told him I hadn't wanted him to correct the essay. I obviously should have clued him in earlier about the way I'd been learning to view and respond to Charlotte's work. Because I hadn't, Charlotte wound up feeling crestfallen, and Tom felt disappointed and shot down. Lesson learned (again): we needed always to work in concert concerning Charlotte's LD.

GAINING PERSPECTIVE

During that year, Charlotte's school offered a program for parents aimed at giving them some perspective on what their LD children were dealing with every day. I jumped at the opportunity. It turned out to be one of the most eye-opening experiences I've had throughout this whole LD journey.

That night, a bunch of parents of Churchill students gathered to learn to see through our children's eyes. This was a room full of high-powered, successful people. We were all sort of timid at the beginning. We were afraid that we were going to be made to look foolish, and *we were made to look foolish*. That's a big part of our kids' experience—they feel foolish in what seem like normal, everyday situations.

Over the course of the evening, we had to try things like writing a sentence on an index card that we held to our chest, using our left hand, moving from left to right; and writing a composition, but without using the letter "S" even once. I tell you, it felt like having your legs cut off or being bound and gagged. Here we all were, these so-called achievers. We all wanted to do it "right," but we couldn't. It was a set of completely foreign feelings for most of us and such an important glimpse into our children's experiences.

In my mind, I knew what I wanted to write, but I couldn't form the letters clearly. I couldn't find the words I wanted, either. I was conscious of my peers, wondering if they had done it better. The harder I tried, the messier my letters got. The more rushed I felt, the more my hand wouldn't obey my mind. The thoughts were inside me, but locked inside me. I felt stifled, imprisoned, locked in. And the only ideas I was communicating to the teacher were in messy scribble. This was a big lesson.

I came away from that evening with so much. Through each of the many exercises, it took all my concentration to do what the teacher told us to do. I got to see how hard Charlotte has to struggle. I understood what it was like to know in your mind what you want to say but to have a hard time saying it because some part of your brain is not cooperating. I knew how it felt to have my writing sound unintelligent and not up to the level of the thoughts behind it. I was suddenly aware of the sense of utter powerlessness, the frustration, the anguish these kids face day after day in school. I got a taste of their despair and their shame.

And here it was, the end of Charlotte's school years. How I wished I had had this experience sooner.

THE FINE LINE BETWEEN
COACHING AND ENABLING

That evening, I gained so much compassion for Charlotte, I only wanted to make her life easier in any way I could.

When you have a child who is struggling in any way, as a parent, your natural inclination is to try to make things easier. Needless to say, this is not always the best solution. But it's very tricky for parents of LD kids. There's a fine line between helping and enabling—or, more accurately, crippling through enabling. I've learned that kids with LD have a lot of fears and self-doubt, and if you give in to their first rumblings about how they just "can't" do this or that, you'll send them the message that they truly can't and shouldn't even try, lest they face certain humiliation.

This dilemma presents itself over and over for me, even today. I have found that I am often wondering whether and how much to help, in one situation after another. It's difficult to make hard-and-fast rules about what you will and will not do because different circumstances dictate different actions. A parent's behavior in one situation may be helpful, and the same behavior on a different day, in a different situation, may be enabling. And, of course, things change over time; something that was supportive when Charlotte was a small child might be crippling for her when she's older.

When Charlotte was first diagnosed, I can admit that I wasn't very supportive. I was loving but not effective in expressing that love by giving her what she needed. I felt despair that I knew so little of what LD meant and what I should do. So, even though I felt great warmth, great love, and a desire to hold, to cuddle, to comfort, to "mother," at the same time, I felt at a loss for the best way to help her (and me) navigate the coming years.

As I learned more and more about LD and about what it must be like to be Charlotte—to feel confused and disorganized when others didn't—I wanted desperately to help. My first impulse, and I imagine this happens to the majority of parents, was to do things for her. "Oh, zipping her jacket is so hard for her. Let me do it so she won't be frustrated." As I've confessed, sometimes—not always—it was more like, "Let me do it so we won't be late."

Tom and I both still struggle with the inclination to do things for Charlotte instead of just guiding her or letting her figure them out on her own. When Charlotte was a senior in high school, she called Tom one morning from the local subway station to tell him the train wasn't running. He said, "Well, Charlotte, get in a cab, and go to school." Charlotte told him she didn't have any money with her. Then he said, "Well, Charlotte, walk to school." And she said she didn't know how to get there. She had walked home from school but never to school; for her, there is a big difference. Finally, Tom said, "Come back up to the loft, and I'll give you money for a cab."

Later, he realized that he should not have moved in quite so quickly to "save" her in the situation. Instead, he might have said, "Charlotte, try to figure it out. Ask people for directions uptown, and you'll get there." Indeed, that likely would have worked: one of Charlotte's saving graces is her ability to appeal to people and get help from them.

And what if Tom hadn't been there to help her? What would she have done then? She's going to have to be able to fend for herself in the real world. Instead of letting Charlotte learn how to handle this on her own and find her way, Tom offered her a quick and easy solution.

I know that Charlotte would have been fine—and probably better off—if Tom hadn't quickly solved the problem. I know this because a little more than a year before that, Charlotte had gotten stuck in the subway during a New York City blackout. When the lights went out, she was underground. It was dark and scary, and no one knew what was happening. Charlotte started to cry, and a woman nearby her became her instant ally. A little later, a police officer helped her to get off the train and out of the Fourteenth Street station.

Once Charlotte was out in the muggy summer daylight, she had to figure out where she was and how to get to my office on Forty-first Street. I had been waiting for her there. She talked to people, and they pointed her in the right direction. And much to my surprise, Charlotte found her way to me. Charlotte, who has extreme difficulty with directions, who doesn't understand numbers and numbered streets, wended her way through the throngs of other lost New Yorkers that day, appealing to people with her charm all along the path.

Now, if there hadn't been a blackout, and I had said to Charlotte, "Take the train to Fourteenth Street and then find my office," she would have simply said, "I can't do that."

THAT'S LIFE

There are certain aspects of having LD—or being different in any way, really—that no amount of parental understanding, coaching, or consoling can undo. You can talk and talk and talk, and maybe your child will feel better for the moment, but there will always be new experiences that reinforce a feeling of being "less" than everyone else.

A case in point: Charlotte had been feeling pretty good about herself and her future at the beginning of her senior year of high school. But at our Thanksgiving dinner that year, she came face to face again with feelings of inadequacy.

Every Thanksgiving we have a big dinner of about twenty-five to thirty people. Tom cooks, and I take a bunch of people to watch the Macy's parade from my office window overlooking Broadway. At that year's dinner, college was a major topic of conversation. Our guests, close friends and relatives, naturally thought it would be an easy conversation opener, given that Charlotte was a senior and Annie a junior in high school.

They asked Charlotte about it mostly. Where did she plan to go? What did she plan to study. These are heavily loaded questions for any kid, let alone a kid whose choices are limited to special schools and those that offer special LD programs. To make matters worse, one of our houseguests, the son of a long-time friend, was applying to Brown, Yale, and other Ivy League schools. So, what was already a set of loaded questions now had an added, painful twist. It didn't help that Annie, as a junior two years younger than Charlotte, was beginning to think about colleges, mostly top-notch schools as well. The conversation was easier for her than for Charlotte.

But before the conversation ever unfolded, Charlotte anticipated it and was a mess. Just before our guests were to arrive, around 5:00 p.m., I found her lying in my dressing room in the fetal position and a puddle of tears.

Terrified, I kneeled down to ask her what was going on.

"It makes me sad when the conversation turns to Ivy League, so-called top-notch schools," she said. "People ask where I'm applying and I say, 'Curry College, Mitchell College,' and they say 'Where's that?' And you're telling me that these colleges are fine, they're good, that I can get an education at all different types of schools. But other people don't think that. They just want to hear about the Big Ones. Plus, I just looked in a book about LD programs at colleges and found out that my SAT scores are bad. I didn't know. I thought they were ok. But they're not."

I then went through the talk that Charlotte and I know so well: "Charlotte, you know the SAT doesn't measure all types of intelligence, and there are thousands of other colleges than the Harvards and Yales. Most people don't go to Ivy League schools."

But in spite of my brave talk—which had become almost ritualistic because Charlotte and I had talked through all these arguments before—she was still hurting. The hurt, the disappointment of not being able to compete on the playing field, runs very, very deep. It's sad, unfair, and frustrating, and it will always be there. It doesn't mean that Charlotte can't come to terms with it, but it will always be there in her life.

EXCUSES, EXCUSES

As Charlotte got older and became more articulate in explaining what things felt like, I got a fuller picture of her experience and was able to empathize more. I found myself moving into the role of the nurturer, and it felt good. She'd come home from school and tell me of her anxieties and frustrations. At the beginning, she wasn't able to advocate for herself. I talked with her teachers to help explain what was working in the classroom and what wasn't, as I saw it from home.

Perhaps I was overcompensating for the years when I wasn't as supportive as I should have been, but at a certain point, I think I went too far and became enabling in certain ways of Charlotte's fears and doubts.

We got into the habit of checking in each day after school. We'd sit on the sofas at the front of the loft, often relaxing, lounging next to each other. I'd debrief Charlotte about her day, both socially and academically. "What happened today?" I'd ask her. "How'd you feel?" I was just myself discovering the overwhelming importance of that second question in everyone's life and was very into finding out the answer as a way of getting to know the woman my sweet daughter was growing into.

I realize now that I often let these conversations turn into complaint sessions. She'd paint a picture of her school day as difficult and bleak. Every night, night after night, I'd only hear the complaints, the tales of what didn't work, stories of being left out of a group, or "dissed," or ignored. Not that there weren't good things going on in Charlotte's life. Sometimes there'd be glimmers of good news: some boy threw paper wads at her, or she flirted with so and so a tiny bit. But I'd very rarely come home to an ebullient "Wow, listen to this!"

Once, when she was in eleventh grade, I was at a meeting with her principal, and I spotted Charlotte between classes. She was laughing and chatting and bouncing along with a whole group of chattering friends. I had never seen that. *Ever.* I was speechless. I asked the principal whether she was always like that; he looked surprised that I was asking and said, "Yeah."

I began to see that our relationship as it was relied on my being the Mother and Nurturer and Charlotte being the Weak Hurt Daughter. She only knew how to capture my attention if she came to me with her disappointments and hurts to take care of. She wanted to keep on looking at the "bad" parts of her life with me so that I would stay with her and keep thinking them through. We often ended up dwelling there way too long.

I couldn't see it at first, but together we were doing what I knew I didn't want the public at large to do: looking at Charlotte as her LD, as someone who is unable and weak. This was reinforcing her insecurities and sadness. By the time we would finish talking or run out of time, Charlotte would have morphed into one mopey bag of bones and learning differences.

I think Charlotte also enjoyed this particular bond between us because it was something Annie didn't have with me. It took longer to hear Charlotte's stories than it did to hear Annie's. Annie could rattle off the thrill in mastering snowboarding in two-minutes flat. But Charlotte's tales of woe—for example, how impossible it was for her to understand graphs and how that lack of understanding destroyed her interest in environmental science and, on top of that, decreased her self-esteem—could go on for more than an hour.

Another thing started happening: Charlotte would fall back on the excuse of her LD as a way of getting out of doing some things. "But I can't," she'd frequently protest, crying, whether the task was cleaning up her room, packing her weekend bag, finding her keys, clearing the dinner table, or folding laundry. And she'd play the sympathy card to try to get attention. If Annie told a story at dinner about something that had upset her that day, before any of us could react, Charlotte was in hysterics because of something that had upset her that day.

It remains an ongoing struggle, knowing when Charlotte can and can't do things and when she's looking for attention or the easy way out. She often doesn't know herself. I suppose some of that is just teenager stuff, not LD stuff. But I've realized I can't simply let her off the hook; it's my job to help her become an accountable member of society.

I tried that with her disaster area of a messy room. No one will ever mistake Charlotte for a neat freak like me. We are polar opposites when it comes to that.

Part of Charlotte's problem with neatness really does come from having LD. It makes it difficult for her to organize things. But part of it seems to be laziness, too. (A friend of mine told me that her LD son jauntily explains his pigpen of a bedroom with, "But, Mom, it's the disease!") I know that LD kids are often unjustly accused of laziness, but I also know that LD kids are human beings, and everyone is lazy some of the time.

Over the years, I've taken different approaches to dealing with Charlotte's room. Early on, I would just go in and clean it myself, a whirling dervish with a trash bag and a bottle of Windex. I would throw out what I saw fit and organize the remaining things into drawers. Later on, I tried sitting on Charlotte's bed and holding things up one at a time, letting her declare yes or no for item after item. This was speedy and efficient, but it didn't produce such a good vibe. Charlotte would want to take her time, deciding the pros and cons of keeping things, and I'd get angry at the slowdown. As I got testy, she'd slow down even more and then lose interest altogether.

The best antidote to the impossibly messy room was when she and I started cleaning and organizing together. This was the most empowering for her. It turns out that, like me, Charlotte gets immense satisfaction out of throwing things away. She gets a much-needed sense of control and mastery when she organizes things in her drawers as she wants them to be. When we cleaned her room together, she would have fun going through old papers, half-used art supplies, old games, whatever, enjoying the memories they called up. The problem was that her stamina was not boundless. Often we'd get to the stage of pulling every thing out and going through about half of it—and then she'd fade. I shouldn't say fade, more like stop dead, over it, done, usually curled up on her bed in exhaustion. And there I was, left facing piles of things that needed to be gone through and restowed.

So, we still haven't found a perfect solution. I worry about Charlotte having trouble keeping roommates because of her messiness, but I suppose she'll really learn the consequences that way, in the real world. And, like she did in the subway during the blackout, she'll figure it out.

Chapter 10

A DIFFERENT
KIND OF GIFTED

A COUPLE OF YEARS AGO, WHEN CHARLOTTE WAS IN
the middle of high school, I brought her to meet my therapist. I
had been talking to Dr. Fischer about her for over a year, just as
I had been talking to Charlotte about him, and I thought it was
a good idea for them to lay eyes on each other.

Well, when he met her, he was shocked.

He couldn't believe the discrepancy between the real Charlotte
and the Charlotte I had described to him. Based on my reports, he
had expected an awkward, spastic, nerdy, needy kid. What he saw
before him instead was a perceptive, intelligent, beautiful, with-it,
and articulate young woman who was incredibly observant of the
world around her.

Boy, had I painted her differently. I had been focused on all
that she couldn't do, all that was negative and frustrating to me

as a mom who still wanted her daughter to be "normal," for her sake and mine. Hearing my therapist's reaction was like having a bucket of cold water splashed on me. I felt like I could suddenly see. It is painful to write about this—it brings me to tears. How could a mother have been so blind?

As far as I'd come, as much progress as I'd made in dealing with Charlotte on a day-to-day basis, I realized that I had fundamentally still been looking at Charlotte through the eyes of a panicked mother who's just learned that her daughter has this thing—this complicated, varied thing that she doesn't understand. I had been looking at Charlotte the same way I had when she was first diagnosed with LD, and it seemed like the end of the world.

I didn't know, in the early days, whether Charlotte would be able to make it through high school or eventually live on her own as an adult. I worried about that all the time, for many, many years. I talked about it in therapy, session after session, and in the process, neglected to mention, let alone really notice, how much the situation, how much Charlotte, had changed.

Over the course of her school years, with lots of help from her special schools, tutors, therapists, me, and the rest of the family, Charlotte had made great strides in every area, much greater strides than I ever thought imaginable. In her final years of school, there was a huge crescendo of achievement. She overcame some long-standing academic hurdles, learned to advocate for herself in the real world, graduated from high school, got accepted to three colleges, and was recognized, publicly, for being a shining example of what it was possible to achieve despite learning differences.

She sure showed me.

FITTING IN

One of the things I was nervous about was how Charlotte would interact with kids who didn't have learning differences. Her whole life, she went to special schools, where all the kids had LD—different types of LD, every one of them. No two cases are the same, but the kids in her schools had similar insecurities and social issues; it was a level playing field, in that way.

But what would happen in the real world, where some kids might be insensitive to people with special needs, or they might not even know what learning differences were? Other than Annie's friends, Charlotte didn't interact much with non-LD kids.

The summer before her senior year in high school, she was selected to attend the National Student Leadership Camp in Colorado, an annual conference of high school student councils from across the country. It was a huge honor. Charlotte was being recognized for her leadership skills, and I was so proud.

At the camp, she was going to be interacting with "normal" kids from all over the country. She wondered whether she should ask her advisor, who'd be on the trip, to tell the counselors and other grown-ups at the camp about her learning differences. She didn't want people who were unfamiliar with LD to pass judgment on her, yet she also didn't want to find herself in situations where there were things she couldn't do, and she'd have to explain why at a crucial or embarrassing moment.

In the end, her advisor told some of the counselors, who frankly really didn't know what to make of the term *learning disabilities*. In a few situations, Charlotte had to stand up and let the kids and counselors know that she had LD and explain what that meant—and it worked out fine. But there was one exercise where they were given a sheet of paper peppered with numbers, printed haphazardly, which they had to categorize. Uh-oh. This is exactly what Charlotte can't do; to her, the world of numbers always looks like that piece of paper or worse—an explosion of random digits just flying off the page.

But Charlotte handled herself beautifully. She took a deep breath and then stated, simply, "I have problems with math and numbers." That might not sound like a big deal to you, but for Charlotte, it was a *huge* deal. It was the first time she told a group of non-LD peers about her differences, and it took a lot of courage. That was one of several personal triumphs for her that week among the non-LD. Charlotte remembers that week very fondly, even though it wasn't always easy, and there were many difficult moments, some of them spent sobbing back in her bunk. It was a week filled with challenges and the kinds of pain that make you grow as a person. Ultimately, it was very empowering for her to get along in the "school of life" and to figure out when she needed to talk about her challenges and when she didn't.

CHOOSING A COLLEGE

Charlotte's experience at the National Student Leadership Camp was a great opportunity for her to see what it might be like to go to a regular college that has a good LD program rather than going to Landmark, the nation's one LD-only college.

Landmark is a two-year school with a wonderful reputation for helping kids with learning differences move on to other colleges for their junior and senior years. Tom and I assumed for a long time that if Charlotte were to go to college, it would be at Landmark. She had only known special schools. Living away from home would be enough of a challenge, we figured. Why add the stress of trying to adjust to being in a non-LD environment?

But Charlotte decided she didn't want to continue to live in an LD-exclusive world anymore. She wanted to enter the "real" world, where people wouldn't know about her LD unless she told them about it.

She had been encouraged by her history teacher, her favorite teacher, Mr. Legrand. He was one of those once-in-a-lifetime, thoroughly dedicated, gifted teachers—young, tireless, funny, enthusiastic, a bundle of energy and humor. Mr. Legrand could rib the guys and joke with the girls. He was the teacher sponsor of the student council that Charlotte was active in, and he was the one who chaperoned her in Colorado at the leadership camp.

Charlotte and Mr. Legrand had a special bond. He inspired her with his presentation of history—like a living, vital story. He was also able to recognize her formidable strengths and pushed her to write better papers, make arguments more clearly, and state her position in front of a group.

While Tom and I were gently pushing Landmark, Mr. Legrand was telling Charlotte, "Don't sell yourself short."

I was angry when I first heard this, and I called the school to talk to the principal to complain about it. How could he position Landmark as a sellout to Charlotte? How could he paint it at "less than" when it seemed to me her only real option—and when I had gone to such trouble to make her feel as if there was no stigma attached to a special school?

But in hindsight, I see he was onto something. He saw in Charlotte what I still wasn't seeing, even at the late date of her senior year of high school. Though I'd come a long way from when she was young, when I was first so bewildered and frightened by her learning differences, I still wasn't able to see her potential for academic viability—the whole Charlotte.

Clearly, Mr. Legrand and Charlotte had a different relationship than Charlotte's and mine. There were no complex "Mom I can't do it, so baby me" dynamics going on to confuse things. Mr. Legrand admired her and inspired her, and she adored him and lived up to his expectations.

Still, she applied to Landmark and got accepted. She also got accepted to two other schools, where they have great LD programs. Toward the end of Charlotte's senior year in high school, I took her on a three-day trip to visit those schools. It was a momentous rite of passage.

The night before we left, Charlotte was anxious and nuts, like a cat on a griddle, unable to get settled, full of fears and anxiety. I was too, but in that symbiosis that has sprung up, I held mine inside, and we both lived through hers. She said she couldn't get comfortable, wasn't going to be able to sleep. Looming big in her mind was the idea that once she left—left home, left the LD world—she could never come back. Suppose she couldn't make it out there? Suppose people were mean? Suppose she couldn't fit in socially in a mainstream world? Suppose she couldn't understand the classes? The college professors wouldn't stop and explain every time she couldn't follow something. What would that feel like? How would she succeed?

I tried to soothe her. I said, "You're going on a shopping trip. You don't have to perform. You don't have to do anything. You don't even have to say anything if you don't want to. You're already accepted. It's the schools that are trying to sell themselves to you. You just have to look, to see if you can imagine yourself being here."

On the designated day, we left at 4:30 a.m. for the drive to New England. Charlotte, knowing herself so well, slept fully clothed so that she could be sure of making it to the car before falling sound asleep for the drive. Hours later, we paused by the side of the road so Charlotte could take off the ratty Harvard sweatshirt that she lives in because it's so soft and yummy, but which we both thought would be inappropriate for a college go-see, and brushed her lovely hair.

"How do I look?' she asked.

"You look just beautiful," I said. There was renewed optimism in her clear, brown eyes.

At the first school, she was met at admissions by an enthusiastic admissions officer. Charlotte pulled out her warm smile and firm, look-'em-in-the-eye handshake that had been winning her praise and admiration all her life. A good-looking male student came to take her to the first class she would sit in on: college writing. After college writing, they would walk around campus and then have lunch with students in the cafeteria. I sat outside in front of the library, in the first sun of April spring, to wait. I found myself reading my work e-mails on my blackberry—a connection to my public, career self—and reading my Trollope novel—a connection to my own college English major self. When Charlotte emerged after lunch, led by a bubbly female freshman, she was radiant. I asked, "How was it?" and she said, "It was great!" The earth trembled. The heavens parted. The angels sang. Things were looking up.

NOT SO SIMPLE MATH

Mr. Legrand had also encouraged Charlotte in her senior year to have another try at the New York State Regents Exam for math, a test she'd failed in her junior year. Each spring, the Regents tests are given in a variety of subjects and are designed to see how well New York State schools are educating their students. Charlotte didn't need to pass Regents exams in order to graduate, and she was already accepted into college, but she couldn't get the prestigious Regents diploma without them, something she wanted desperately.

Still, I wondered about the point of putting herself through an awful standardized test again. In her worst subject.

As I've discussed earlier, there is nothing more troubling for Charlotte than being faced with numbers, in almost any situation. Even in Manhattan, most of which is a numbered grid, Charlotte has trouble finding her way around. She's been known to skip lunch because she can't tell whether the $5 in her pocket is more than the $2.50 it costs for a slice of pizza. She sometimes calls one of us on her cell phone from a taxi to ask how much change she's supposed to ask for.

Math has always been Charlotte's most difficult subject. We've tried everything to remediate that. She even spent time taking the Lindamood Bell remedial math course. But unlike the Lindamood Bell reading course, which helped her tremendously, the math course didn't seem to work.

I was upset when I learned that kids at the Churchill School would have to take Regents exams at all. How could those kids compete with non-LD kids?

Surprisingly, Charlotte passed the biology Regents (she failed the earth science Regents because she didn't see that there was a second page). Even more surprisingly, she failed the one in global history, which is one of her strongest subjects. She failed that one by just one point, even though two teachers plus the principal of the school combed her test to see if they could find that one point she needed.

We knew, like we knew our names, that she didn't have a chance of passing the math Regents the first time she took it. In math class, she was struggling to learn to read simple graphs and had never been able to absorb basic algebra or geometry. Charlotte had by that time taken the math PSAT, on which she had signed her name, answered two questions and then walked out; you get two hundred points for signing in.

Sure enough, when the time for the math Regents came, she flunked. But then, the spring of senior year came, and encouraged by Mr. Legrand, Charlotte decided to take the test again.

Tom and I asked her, "Why would you put yourself through that again?" Who cared about the math Regents? Well, Charlotte did. She made me buy her the math review book. She worked after school with her soft-spoken, brilliant math teacher and coach drilling it in, drilling it in. All I could think was, *When she fails again, she's going to feel bad.*

As the weeks went by, Charlotte was quiet about how it was going, knowing we were puzzled by and not particularly supportive of the whole effort to pass this test that no one outside New York State has ever heard of. The night before the test, she got to sleep earlyish. In the morning, before she went in to school, she was quiet, not complaining, not whining, keeping her own counsel. It was amazing: it took her six hours to complete the test—she gets untimed tests because of her LD—and she didn't give up. When she was done, we spoke on the phone. I asked her how she did, and she said, "I don't know. I probably didn't do that well."

Later that afternoon, I got a call from Charlotte's math teacher saying Charlotte had passed the math Regents. It was a movie moment. I almost dropped the phone. "What?" I begged. "Charlotte passed the math."

Tom was out of town, and when we spoke later in the day, I asked if he'd heard. Yes, Mr. Nagubandi had called him on his cell phone; when he heard, he had cried.

For the next several days, Charlotte became larger than life in our eyes. She seemed totally different to us, this girl who passed the math Regents. The whole Churchill faculty, including the principal, were in awe. No one could stop talking about this miracle.

PUMPS AND CIRCUMSTANCE

Charlotte's high school graduation in June of 2005 turned out to be one of the most wonderful, most emotional days our family has ever experienced. At one time, I thought I'd never see that day. The year leading up to it had brought so many triumphs for Charlotte, academically, socially, and emotionally. We were all really on a high.

Combined with that was a certain grief every mother probably feels when her baby, her first baby, walks to the podium and receives her diploma. From the moment I awoke, at 6:30 a.m., I felt it. It was the end of Charlotte's childhood, and there was a ceremony to mark it. She would no longer be my full-time charge. My identity as Charlotte's handler, guide, therapist, mentor, mom would be over by 1 p.m. that day. I felt a bit empty, obsolete, like a used gasoline can. I burst into tears before I got out of bed.

At 9 a.m., I took a cab with Charlotte to New York University, where the graduation ceremony was to be held. I took in Charlotte's beauty in the sunlight. She was wearing a purple and black ministriped Lycra number, form fitting with a very scooped neck, and my gold Manolo Blahniks (borrowed only for rare occasions, mind you!). I felt the tears again. I called Tom and asked him to bring tissues, sensing, foreseeing a possible faucet effect coming on during the ceremony. Charlotte's hair was sopping wet from her shower, so I reached across and fluffed it and opened the taxi window so the wind could help dry it. "Mom!" she protested. She was still a teenager.

Once we got to NYU, Charlotte went to don her cap and gown, and I hung out in the auditorium, waiting. There, I bumped into the headmistress of the school. We had had our differences over the years, mainly about dress code. What high school girl needed to be wearing collared shirts with sleeves every day? In New York City, no less. Today, though, there was no talk of such things. We hugged. And she inadvertently gave me a hint of the wonderful moment that was to come a little later on.

She looked me in the eye and said, "We are so proud of Charlotte. Especially for today." A tingle went through my body. What did she mean? There was no valedictorian. I had heard they were giving out one award at the graduation ceremony, only one . . . I suddenly felt full of expectation, and I had an eerie sense of wonder and awe.

I have always been a sit-in-the-front-row girl. As if it were a sign to me, an omen for Charlotte's future, there were enough seats in the front row to accommodate the people who would come to witness Charlotte's big moment. Tom teases me and gets exasperated when I run ahead to get front-row seats or the "best" seats when we're out. And here, on the morning that I'd resolved not to rush or try for them, they were waiting for us.

I felt happy and excited as parents I knew filed into the rest of the seats, talking, greeting, hugging. After four years of being in the same boat, most likely we'd never see each other again. I hadn't known any very well; I had only alluded to my fears and frustrations to a few and had had more confiding moments with a couple. But I never poured my heart out to any.

Then, Tom and Annie arrived, then Monica, the grandparents, my niece Petra. We were all so expectant. Internally, I was chewing over what the head of the school had said to me about being especially proud of Charlotte today. I knew there was the one award. I went back and forth between not setting myself up for disappointment by allowing myself to think she was getting this award and being absolutely certain she was getting it.

I wondered if I should tell Tom about what I was thinking. I didn't want to ruin a potential surprise for him. But weren't we working on learning to share everything now? I went over and whispered in his ear, "I think Charlotte is getting the big award."

He asked, "Why do you think that?"

I told him what the head of the school said, and Tom responded, "I don't know. I'm not going to get my hopes up."

All of a sudden, the ceremony started with a very loud recorded rendition of "Pomp and Circumstance." I had chills, prickles on my neck, a flutter in my blood. The graduates walked in two by two. There they came down the aisle, with their beautiful young skin and shy smiles. There came Charlotte, radiant, in her blue polyester cap and gown and yellow rosebud corsage.

After they were all seated, the ceremony began. It was a comfortably predictable ritual, very formal, traditional. They began presenting the diplomas, calling names. One by one, the kids came up for a handshake and a hug with the five luminaries on the stage. When Charlotte's turn came, there was extra applause. She stumbled on her way up the stairs just as she has all her life. But that was okay—she just laughed and kept on going. We all applauded for her, the way that everyone else applauded for their kids.

After all thirty-two graduates had accepted their diplomas, the applause died down. The principal of the school, Glenn Corwin, got up again.

He started, "The Winston Churchill Award is presented today to one of our graduating seniors in honor of outstanding contributions made to . . ." I realized that this was it. I quit breathing so I could hear every word. I looked at Tom and Annie, at our whole contingent of eight listening rapturously. The whole auditorium was attentive, focused, quiet. Who? Who? Who is it?

He went on, ". . . an important leader of the student council, member of athletic teams . . ." My mind was flip-flopping: *It's Charlotte. It's not Charlotte. It's Charlotte.* "Most importantly today's recipient demonstrated respect, kindness and sensitivity . . . true citizenship, leadership and courage. . . ." I looked over at Tom and Annie. They seemed as alert and excited as I was.

Glenn kept talking and talking, ". . . proud to present this award to Charlotte Farber."

I felt unbelievable release and joy. I looked over, and Tom's eyes were red, tears streaming down his face. Annie was also crying joyful tears.

I heard the applause of the whole auditorium as Charlotte stood. She gave a spontaneous skip of pleasure and went up the steps to receive the award. I get tingly again as I recall the whole event. I looked at Tom, and he looked back at me and smiled. I looked around at our whole group of supporters of Charlotte in her journey—we were all tears and smiles.

This award meant so much to me, to Charlotte, to all of us. It made me so proud, but that's not all. It made me feel confident in my daughter in a way I hadn't before. It felt like a sign that she was going to be all right, that things were going to be all right.

This was not an award for being disabled; this was an award for being excellent, superior, worthy of special mention. This was a sort of public validation that was completely new to Charlotte.

REALITY CHECK

Just before Charlotte went off to her freshman year of college, I found myself back in the old days. Packing was the task at hand, and, of course, Charlotte and I approach this task rather differently. I came home from work, and, sure enough, Charlotte's room looked like a bomb had hit it. And at the same time that she was packing, she was trying to bake some premixed cookie dough and couldn't understand why nothing was happening to it. Lo and behold, she was pressing the wrong button on the stove.

To me, this was utter chaos, and despite seven years of therapy and all that I had supposedly learned, this pushed all my buttons. I felt overwhelmed and angry, and Charlotte felt hurt that I was angry. And there we were. Charlotte was regressing. And so was I.

Then, I took a look at Charlotte's yearbook and found Mr. Legrand's inscription in it. It was something about how, wasn't it funny that time when they were shopping and she dropped everything, but she still kept her cool? He went on to praise her enthusiasm and courage, her poise and optimism, and I started to cry. Mr. Legrand knew how to embrace Charlotte's LD and her clumsy nature; he knew how to nurture her and encourage her without becoming short-tempered. Why, after all this time, wasn't this second nature for me?

It began to dawn on me. It's just a really difficult thing being an LD mom. On the one hand, you have to nurture and accept and enfold your child in limitless love, wrap warm arms around her and tell her that she's the best, the finest, the most wonderful being that ever lived. On the other hand, you have to be alert to how she's doing, assess what can be remediated, encourage, cajole, pull, push. And all the time, you're the mom, with all your own baggage and hopes and dreams and faults and foibles and history and love. Teachers don't have the baggage of the parental relationship, the personal complications and mess that make it all seem impossible.

All this is to say that even though I've learned a lot, I am not perfect. And even though Charlotte has come very, very far and won a big award, neither is she.

A SHINING EXAMPLE

Charlotte received the Winston Churchill Award at her high school graduation because she was a great example for other kids to follow. She tries hard, she is honest and just, she's learned to speak up for herself, she's compassionate, and she's a great leader.

At home, too, she's been a great example for all of us to follow in many ways—and most of the time we haven't even known it.

If it weren't for Charlotte, I would never have been pushed to get in touch with my real feelings and learned to live in a way that is true to myself, even if that means revealing my vulnerabilities. I might never have come to appreciate slowing down and being in the moment.

There's so much the family has learned and gained from Charlotte and her experience as a child with LD. For myself, as well as Annie and Tom, it has challenged—and changed—certain assumptions we held about the world and ourselves.

The three of us are high achievers. We're all pretty accustomed to being around people who are very academically oriented. When you travel in that sort of circle, it's very easy to have a pretty narrow view of what intelligence is and what success means.

If Charlotte had been just like Tom, Annie, and me, our worldview, and our tolerance for people unlike ourselves, would have remained very limited. Tom recently expressed to me how much awareness he has gained from having a child who is unlike him in many ways, a child with learning differences. He said, "Watching Charlotte grow up, I've seen how in this culture we put way too much emphasis on achieving and performing. You're always being judged on what schools you go to, what you do, how much you earn—rather than just being."

Annie might not have the compassion she does for kids who can't pick up new skills as naturally as she does if it weren't for having a sister with LD. I might not have realized how important emotional intelligence is—way more important than academic intelligence, if you ask me—if I hadn't had this child whose learning challenges gave her incredible psychological insight and empathy.

A BRIGHT HORIZON

When Charlotte was diagnosed, as you know by now, I certainly didn't think, "Oh, excellent, this is going to be a fun and interesting learning opportunity." But now that her childhood years are over, now that she's sort of off on her own, starting her life independent of her childhood family, it has dawned on me that this experience had been a multilayered one, filled with surprises. The biggest surprise of all has been that there have been great advantages to having a child who has learning differences. It has added a lot of richness, closeness, and opportunities for self-reflection. It's given our family a chance to look at our values and the values of the world.

I will never say that this journey has been easy. It has challenged each of us in the family in every possible way, pushed every one of our individual and collective buttons, forced us to rethink everything we thought we knew, and confronted us emotionally. But for all of that, each of us is truly better off. It *has* been a great gift, in many ways. From where I stand now, I wouldn't trade this experience.

When this book hits stores, Charlotte will be a freshman in college. I have no idea what she'll be studying, what kinds of grades she'll earn, what she'll be when she grows up. I'm sure she'll go through some major adjustments—some just like those of every freshman away at college for the first time and others that only an LD kid in a non-LD world for the first time can relate to.

Of course, in some ways, I'm nervous. Any parent sending her child—her baby, who was once six pounds, nine ounces—off to college feels this. I also feel a bit anxious about where she's going to end up: not only in college but also after. I wonder about Charlotte's future, what kinds of jobs she'll be able to do, if she'll ever be able to handle driving. LD never goes away; it will be with her always, even though she'll be able to compensate for it in many ways.

But time will tell. Charlotte has come farther than I ever expected her to, and there's a part of me now that feels confident she'll lead a great life—one that she likes, that isn't rushed and cluttered.

I am so proud of Charlotte. When I think of how far she has come, my heart melts. When I think of how far I have come, I'm excited and grateful to have had the journey.

AFTERW✸RD

Charlotte in Her Own Words

I WAS IN BED ONE NIGHT, ABOUT TO GO TO SLEEP, when my mom came in and told me she was going to write a book about our experience with learning differences. I was so excited, I could barely sleep. I was glad there would finally be a book out there that told the whole story.

There are already many books out there about LD, but most of them don't tell you what it's really like for the kids or the parents—both the bad and the good. And some of the books seem really negative to me. They don't talk about all the ways LD kids can do well, and our strengths. With books like those out there, I can see why kids being diagnosed with LD wouldn't want anyone to know. It's made to seem so bad.

This would be a book that other parents and LD kids could relate to—and so could other people. I would love it if they read the book too, people who don't have learning differences, even though they might never understand it. By the way, I say *learning differences* instead of *learning disabilities* because the word "disability" makes it seem like we're not capable of learning. But we are—we just need to have things taught to us differently because our brains are wired differently. Sometimes, though, I have to live with the "disability" label so that I can get special considerations, like untimed tests.

But I hate the word "disability." It makes some people think having LD means you're not smart at all, or academically flawed. I've seen the reactions on some people's faces when I've told them about my differences. They look really confused and don't know what to say. Or they say dumb things, like, "So, does that mean you're stupid?" I mean, do I *look* stupid? I feel like telling them, "You would never know I was an LD kid if I didn't tell you."

Well, okay, if I'm totally honest, I can see why some people might think that, at times, like when they catch me going in the wrong direction or being completely disorganized. My locker in high school was a big mess, and when I'd open it, papers would fly out. It's what I called "the Charlotte tornado" when friends or teachers would try and help me with it.

So, yeah, there are things that my learning differences make difficult for me that most people take for granted. Like being able to measure with a ruler, which to me may as well be a blank stick because of my problems with math and numbers. Or knowing which basket to shoot the ball in during a basketball game. I once scored points for the other team because I have issues with spatial relations, and went the wrong way.

It's those sorts of things that make me feel humiliated in public, and make me want to hide and not try. I have been working on getting over that, and trying anyway. Part of that is getting comfortable with telling people I have LD, and asking for help when I need it. That would be a lot easier if LD wasn't this subject that no one talked about. I wish people talked about it more. It would seem less like a secret or a big deal. It's like sex—it's in the shhhhh box.

I have been having more and more positive experiences with telling people lately. In my last year of high school, I was at Barnes & Noble, looking for *The Great Train Robbery* for my English class. I had misplaced the school copy and had to replace it. I asked the woman at the information desk where I could find it. She looked it up in the computer, and then told me, "Look in the back, two aisles down." At least that was what I thought she said. So I went and looked. And I looked, and I looked. But my difficulties with directions and organization combined to make it really hard for me.

I could have just given up, and at one time, I would have. But on this day, I went back to the woman at the information desk. I kind of chuckled and said, "Um, I have problems with directions, and I was wondering if you could help me find the book." I was half expecting her to look at me as if I had green scales and twenty-five heads, like some people have. But she didn't. She seemed to know about learning differences. She said, "Sure, come with me," and helped me find it. I wish more people were like her.

When I went to Colorado to a leadership camp with "normal" kids, my experience was not as easy. I was really nervous before I went. We were going to be doing these "team-building" exercises, which I was afraid would reveal my differences.

Some of my worst nightmares did come true there. I cried several times, when I got humiliated because there were things I couldn't understand or do well. There were many times when I wanted to quit, just give up. But what's great is that I got through those moments, I spoke up, and I learned to be really strong. I also climbed a mountain there. You might think, whoop-de-do, but for me it was difficult, and my friend even got hurt on the way down. But that's really what we all do internally — climb mountains, try to get through the struggles one step at time.

During a discussion session at the camp about diversity in our schools, the topic of learning differences came up. This one girl said she felt bad for the special-ed kids in her school, because they got picked on and teased, and they looked up to the so-called normal kids.

I couldn't contain myself. I said, "I have LD. I go to a special school for special education." The room got very quiet. I wanted her to see that I was just like her, except I struggled with academics. She, and the other kids, hadn't known I was different. I think they got to see that LD is not exactly what they thought it was — that kids with LD can be just like them in many ways. We're more like the other kids than they even know: kids got picked on even in my high school, where everyone had LD. Some people even used the word "retard" to hurt other people's feelings. Teenagers can be really mean, with or without LD.

As you can see, kids with LD deal with a lot on top of their difficulty learning — self-consciousness, anxiety. Having to take standardized tests like the SAT even though the odds are stacked against us, having to come up with an answer when someone casually asks how we did on the SAT or where we're going to college. I'm not going to one of the name-brand colleges everyone has heard of. When I tell people where I am going, I try to say it with a lot of confidence. But I realize that most people won't recognize it, and that makes me a little embarrassed, even though I know I should not compare myself to mainstream kids, or to my sister, who takes AP courses and will probably go to one of the top ten colleges in the country.

I feel for my sister, too. It must be hard for her, taking all these intense classes, applying to the name-brand schools, and then feeling restrained about discussing colleges and grades in front of her LD sister. Fortunately, LD doesn't always get in our way. We have close talks about guys and how our day went. We go to the movies, and one time we were having so much fun together there, we *both* almost stepped on the up escalator when we wanted to go down. We get along really well. I love Annie Rose.

Still, there are times when I am very angry at my LD. I want to be able to understand certain things—like algebra—and I want it all to just be easy, and it isn't. That's so frustrating!

But there is another side to it. I've come to accept my LD as just part of who I am. Not only that; I feel like there are good things about it—little things and big things.

For instance, I can read backwards. One day when I was young and having trouble reading, I was in the car with my family when a neon yellow van was behind us. "Ambulance," I said. And my parents looked surprised. The word was written backwards on the front of the ambulance—that way people can read it through their rear-view mirrors. But I was looking at it straight on, and read it backwards. Pretty cool, huh?

But more importantly, LD has made me more sensitive to other people's struggles, and not just other kids with learning differences. It has made me very aware of myself and forced me to pay attention to things in a way I might not have if I had had it easier. It has made me try harder, and, as Winston Churchill once said, "Never, never, never give up."

Just because you have learning differences doesn't mean you can't prosper. Kids with LD are like flowers. How they are nurtured determines how they'll grow. If their spirits are really supported and motivated, those kids can really bloom.

I know because I was nurtured, supported, and motivated by my mother, my father, and my sister, and I have really bloomed, especially in the last couple of years. I don't know what I would have been able to do without my very encouraging family. Without them, my life would be a constant frustration.

I can't believe everything I was able to do at the end of high school—getting into three colleges, graduating from high school, winning the Winston Churchill Award. These are all things I wasn't sure I could do, and, I think, neither were my parents. I even got up the confidence to try the math Regents again with encouragement from some of my teachers. I was in the lowest math class in my grade, so I knew it was going to be really hard. It took me a long time to finish—I was the last to leave the room. Afterward, my teacher came outside to talk to me and told me, yes, I had passed! I didn't even need to take the test again since I was already accepted to college, but it was a big triumph for me, representing the population of those who have difficulty with math, and getting a New York State Regents diploma.

Graduation day was the most incredible day of all for me. I couldn't believe I got that far! Suddenly, it felt as if high school was over in a snap.

Before the procession, I was in this room with all the other kids from my class. I realized that I would not see many of them again. Maybe every once in a while, but this would be the last meeting with our entire grade, the year 2005 class. That made me feel a bit sad. I was also starting to feel nervous about college.

We were given our royal blue gowns and caps with yellow tassels—what a strange hat, I thought. I wasn't the only one who had a hard time figuring out how to wear it. Underneath my gown, I wore a really tight, striped Betsey Johnson dress, and my mom even let me wear her gold Manolos. I felt like Dorothy in *The Wizard of Oz*.

I was really nervous through the whole procession and ceremony, but I got extra nervous when the principal, Mr. Corwin, started to introduce the Winston Churchill Award. It was like there was techno music going in my head. He was describing this person who won the award, and it sounded a lot like me. But I thought, *Nah. It couldn't be me.*

And then, he announced my name, "CHARLOTTE FARBER." I couldn't believe I got the award. I suddenly felt like I was in a movie. I was thrilled, and I couldn't stop smiling. It was amazing. When I got off the stage, I went across to sit back down, and saw my whole family crying. Wow. I could feel how proud they were of me.

It was the perfect end to my last year of high school. I had learned and achieved so much that year. I guess it's because I put in so much effort at Churchill that I got so much out of it. That experience molded me into a person I want to be.

Receiving that award on graduation day was also a great new beginning for me. It made me feel like I am not just my LD. And it made me feel as if I can do anything, in college and beyond. There is so much I want to do. Sometimes I think about being an artist or a fashion designer like my mom. But then, I think of how my teachers have helped me, and I think I might want to help kids who have LD in some way, to make a difference in someone's life, change the world a little bit.

That last one is a strong possibility. I've been very lucky because New York City has many good schools for kids with LD. But I'm aware that this is not true everywhere and that many LD kids in New York can't afford to go to the special schools I attended. This makes me sad. I have heard stories from high school friends of mine who used to go to regular schools about what it was like to be "mainstreamed." They didn't get all the attention they needed, which is why they made a change and came to my school. (They also had a hard time with the "normal" kids and never really fit in.)

I wish that, across the country, at all economic levels, kids with LD could have the opportunity to get the special education they need, in both public and private schools. Maybe some day I can help with that. Maybe I can help make sure LD kids everywhere get the help and attention they need to get a fair chance in life.

You can help with that, too. If you are a child with LD, or a parent of one, please learn from our experience. Don't walk alone with LD. Get tested—it is so worthwhile. Everyone deserves a fair chance. Don't be afraid or embarrassed. It's the only way for a child with LD to get the education he or she needs. And, parents, remember to tell your LD kids that you love them. See the other parts of them, including the things they do well, and point them out. They deserve that.

Who knows, really, what I will end up doing. That is a long way off. I can only tell you that it will be something that I am passionate about and that I will try my best.

— Charlotte Farber

RES✺URCES

Today, there are many resources available to LD kids and their parents. Here are some that I highly recommend.

ORGANIZATIONS

National Center for Learning Disabilities (www.NCLD.org). This is a wonderful organization that provides easy access to information about every aspect of LD, as well as other LD resources. The group is involved in advocacy and education policy as well.

All Kinds of Minds (www.allkindsofminds.org). This is an organization founded and run by brilliant pediatrician Mel Levine, M.D., author of several key books on LD (see below), who is a pioneer of the idea that different children learn in different ways. The organization offers all sorts of programs for students—from testing and evaluation to designing ways to help them learn. There are also programs designed to help teachers understand the many different kinds of minds they might find in their class-rooms and how to reach them.

BOOKS

All Kinds of Minds: A Young Student's Book about Learning Abil-ities and Learning Disorders, by Mel Levine (Educators Publish-ing Service, 1993)

A Mind at a Time, by Mel Levine (Simon & Schuster, 2002)

No Easy Answers: The Learning Disabled Child at Home and at School, by Sally Smith (Bantam, 1995)

Learning Outside the Lines, by Jonathan Mooney and David Cole (Fireside, 2000)

The Survival Guide for Teenagers with LD, by Rhoda Cummings, Ed.D., and G Fisher, Ph.D. (Free Spirit Publishing, 1993)

It's So Much Work to Be Your Friend: Helping the Child with Learning Disabilities Find Social Success, by Richard Lavoie (Touchstone, 2005)

VIDEOS

How Difficult Can This Be? The F.A.T. City Workshop, Eagle Hill Foundation, Inc. (PBS Video, 1989). This video provides a glimpse of what it's like to have learning differences.